*The American
Immigration Collection*

The
Russian Immigrant

JEROME DAVIS

Arno Press and The New York Times

NEW YORK 1969

THE RUSSIAN IMMIGRANT

THE MACMILLAN COMPANY
NEW YORK · BOSTON · CHICAGO · DALLAS
ATLANTA · SAN FRANCISCO

MACMILLAN & CO., LIMITED
LONDON · BOMBAY · CALCUTTA
MELBOURNE

THE MACMILLAN CO. OF CANADA, LTD.
TORONTO

The RUSSIAN IMMIGRANT

BY

JEROME DAVIS, Ph. D.

Sometime Gilder Fellow in Sociology
at Columbia University
Assistant Professor of Sociology
at Dartmouth College

New York
THE MACMILLAN COMPANY
1922

To the Russian workingmen whose unstinted toil helps to maintain the basic industrial mechanism of America, but who for the most part are by this very service kept out of reach of the warm, friendly heart of our people.

PREFACE

SOCIOLOGY must begin its investigations with observation. As Dr. Giddings says of it, "Description and history will keep well in advance of explanation." [1] Of such a study as *The Russian Immigrant*, this is especially true. Moreover, this subject does not readily lend itself to adequate statistical treatment—the data thus far collected by our Federal Government are too meager, and to attempt an independent investigation would involve large resources and an extensive organization. The present monograph is an attempt to describe only the main social forces impinging on the Russian in America, and their inevitable effect on his mind.

Of many shortcomings in this treatise, the writer is very much aware. At best it can be but an approximation of conditions among the majority of Russians in this country. The reader must bear in mind that the research was made during a period when the Russian's attitude was affected by the great social upheaval in his native land, and must remember that in America one result of the war spirit was a series of repressive measures against aliens, especially Russians.

[1] Giddings, F. H., *The Principles of Sociology* (New York, 1916), p. 54.

Since the bulk of the Russian immigration to the
United States is made up of the peasant and working classes, it is with them that we are chiefly concerned. By Russian, as used here, is meant the
Great Russian, inhabiting Central Russia; the White
Russian, living between Poland and Russia; and the
Little Russian, from what was formerly South Russia. It does not include the Jews, Poles, Finns,
Letts, Lithuanians, Ruthenians from Galicia, or
other Slavic races. Throughout this study we shall
refer to the Russian group defined above as Russians or Russian Slavs interchangeably.

The method employed has been as follows: First,
the printed matter available on the Russians in
America was analyzed. A partial list of books,
pamphlets, and government reports used is to be
found in the appendix.[2] Second, unpublished materials, the result of surveys made by others, were
utilized. Among these were researches by Mr. Cole
of Chicago, by the Russian Division of the Foreign

---

[2] The only book which the author found dealing exclusively with
immigrants from the Russian empire was a paper-bound volume
entitled *The Russians in America,* which dealt with Jews and
Poles as well as the Russian Slavs and was available only in
the Russian language. The author, Mr. Vilchur, was formerly
editor of *The Russkoye Slovo,* a Russian newspaper printed in New
York. His book is more in the nature of a popular historical sketch
than of an analysis of the relationship of the Russian to our
American society. In addition to this, there was a pamphlet in
Russian, *On the Question of the Organization of the Russian Colony,*
the result of a study made by E. I. Omeltchenko, a member of the
Extraordinary Russian Mission sent to the United States by
Kerensky in 1917. This contains the results of personal visits to
the various Russian colonies, and the conclusions reached are
important.

Language Governmental Information Bureau, by the
Carnegie Foundation, by the Inter-Racial Council,
and by Mr. Sack of the Russian Information Bureau. Third, a personal investigation of Russian
groups in the United States was made. The writer
was particularly fortunate in having had the background of two years and a half in Russia and a
knowledge of the Russian language, without which
this study would have been impossible. He personally visited the following cities, each one being
the headquarters of a district of the Russian Greek
Orthodox Church in America: New York, including Brooklyn; Bridgeport and Hartford, Conn.;
Boston, Philadelphia, Scranton, Olyphant, Coaldale,
Pittsburgh, Donora, in Pennsylvania; Cleveland,
Detroit, Chicago, Minneapolis. Others he visited
were Ansonia, Waterbury, Seymour, and New Haven, Conn.; Braddock and McKees Rocks, Pa.;
Akron, Ohio; and Denver. Among Russians in the
states of North Dakota, Washington, and California, special investigations were made on a uniform
basis, and the detailed reports were incorporated
with those gained by personal investigation. In
each of the communities the leaders of the various
Russian groups were interviewed. These included
any or all of the following: (a) the Russian priests,
(b) the Russian consul, (c) the editors of Russian papers, (d) Russian professional men, (e)
Russian workmen or farmers. Where possible,
visits were made to observe: (a) workmen's clubs,

(b) Russian Socialist or Communist party headquarters, (c) typical homes of Russian workmen including boarding houses. In some cases, conferences were held with the following American agencies when they were doing work for Russians: (a) American churches, (b) Americanization committees, (c) industrial or Americanization Y.M.C.A. secretaries, (d) International Institutes of the Y.W.C.A., (e) banks, (f) labor union officials, (g) employers of Russian labor, (h) public hospitals where Russians are treated, (i) U. S. Immigration officers, (j) teachers or experts who had special contacts with foreigners. Russians imprisoned on Ellis Island and in Hartford were also personally interviewed. Later, with the authorization of the Assistant Secretary of Labor, Mr. Post, the writer talked with over one hundred other Russians imprisoned by the Federal Government in Detroit and Pittsburgh.

The writer wishes to express his appreciation of courtesies extended him in securing copies of letters, documents, and articles from the Foreign Language Governmental Information Bureau, now under the American Red Cross.

He is indebted to the various authors of the Americanization studies of the Carnegie Foundation for original material and for permitting access to advance copies of their manuscripts, and to the Research Department of the National Board of the Young Women's Christian Association for allowing the freedom of their files. He acknowledges the kindness of the United States Department of Labor in having given him every assistance in visiting the prisons where Russians were confined and in furnishing original data. His warmest thanks are due especially to all the Russian individuals and groups too numerous to mention, who gave so generously of their time, and whose coöperation was essential to the completion of the study.

The author is grateful to Dr. Thomas Reed Powell, Dr. Henry R. Seager, Dr. Robert E. Chaddock, Dr. W. F. Ogburn, and Dr. R. S. Woodworth for reading certain chapters or making helpful criticism. He desires also to express his especial appreciation of the assistance of Dr. Alvan A. Tenney. To Dr. Franklin H. Giddings the writer feels under lasting obligation for being the first to open his mind to the deeper implications of sociology and for influencing his thinking on the subject of this study.

The responsibility for the viewpoint taken and for any errors or shortcomings in the treatment, rests on the writer alone.

CONTENTS

PAGE

THE RUSSIAN IMMIGRANT

CHAPTER I

INTRODUCTION: THE RUSSIAN PROBLEM

NEVER before in history has a democratic nation attempted to assimilate such a large and constantly inflowing stream of foreigners as has the United States. In consequence, we have become a heterogeneous nation of mixed races. The thirteenth census tells us that two-fifths of our population are foreign-born. During the war it was found that twenty-four and nine-tenths per cent of the men in the draft camps were illiterate.[1] Unless we can strengthen likemindedness and a sense of national solidarity this situation is pregnant with danger.[2] Following the war the immigration problem has again forced itself on public attention. Congress has for the first time enacted a measure which restricts incoming immigrants to a percentage of the number of the nationals [3] of each country residing here. This effectively stops the flood of foreigners

---

[1] U. S. Bureau of Education, Report of the Commissioner of Education (1919), p. 44.

[2] *Cf.* Giddings, *Inductive Sociology* (N. Y., 1901), pp. 227-8, "The Laws of Liberty."

[3] Nationals here means all persons of foreign birth whether naturalized or not.

who desire to escape the hardships resulting from the World War but affords scant aid to the millions now in the United States. Up to Jan. 1, 1922, Congress had not yet taken any action whatsoever, on any of the bills for the promotion of Americanization.[4] Within the vast aggregation of foreigners already here, each racial group presents its own problems. Among others, those who came from the old empire of the Russian Tsars have attracted particular attention as including within their ranks dangerous alien agitators and Bolshevik agents.

Early in 1920 the Department of Justice took occasion to warn the country of the "red menace," and even sent to the newspapers, at its own expense, plates ready for printing with the following headlines:[5] "Warns Nation of the Red Peril—U. S. Department of Justice Urges Americans to Guard Against Bolshevism Menace." We have only to recall the series of raids instigated by state and national authorities during 1919 and 1920 to appreciate the situation. In New York State the Lusk Committee instituted a vigorous search for "red" aliens, while in the nation at large the Department of Justice conducted raids in which over five thousand were arrested. It now has cards of two hundred thousand ultra-radical individuals and organ-

[4] Letter to the author from the Chief Clerk of the U. S. Bureau of Education.
[5] Dean Pound of the Harvard Law School and eleven other prominent lawyers, *Report Upon the Illegal Practices of the United States Department of Justice* (Washington, 1920), p. 67.

izations in the United States.[6] According to the report of the Attorney General, fully ninety per cent of those considered the most dangerous are aliens.[7] Since the chief targets of these activities were those from the Russian Empire and over ninety per cent of those deported were sent to Russia, it is especially important that we know and understand the Russian Slav in America.

It is true that since many Russians are now voluntarily leaving our country, the problem might seem to be simplified; in reality it thus becomes more complex. For two and one-half years the writer was in intimate contact with soldiers and peasants in many parts of Russia; and he found it difficult to find a peasant or soldier who had been in America and was still friendly to us. Instead, they cursed us as a nation of money-getters and selfish capitalists. The thousands of disappointed and embittered Russians who have already left our shores are doubtless now acting in many cases as agents of hatred, as they go through city, town, and village; they serve to spread the gospel of enmity towards America, and prejudice large numbers of the people against our nation.[8] From the merely selfish standpoint of international trade, this will prove costly; from the standpoint of international peace and mutual understanding it is most deplorable. The activ-

[6] *Report of the Attorney General of the United States, 1920,* p. 173.
[7] *Ibid.,* p. 177.
[8] Professor Petrunkevich of Yale has noted this danger. *Cf. Standard,* Feb., 1920, p. 175.

ity of the American Relief Administration and the appropriation of twenty millions by Congress in December, 1921, for the work of that organization in Russia is helping to counteract this; nevertheless the attitude of the multitude of Russians who have been and are now in America, may in the long run count for more.

Besides these motives there is yet a stronger reason for centering our attention on the Russian Slav. No books in the English language and but meager material describing this one nationality in America are available.[9] Most writers have attempted to analyze conditions as they affect the Russians as a part of a general consideration of the immigrant races, sometimes reviewing but one phase of the problem such as health.[10] In the present study instead of cutting across many racial lines we shall hope to get a cross section, as it were, of the outstanding social forces acting on the one racial group, the Russian. To some extent, however, the experience of the Russian Slav is the experience of all the races from southeastern Europe. Since 1882, the aliens from southeastern Europe, frequently termed the "new immigration," have been growing numerically over those from northwestern Europe in an ever-increasing ratio. A study of the Russian problem, therefore, will have a value for the larger Slavic group as well.

[9] *Cf.* footnote, Preface, p. viii.
[10] See the volumes of the Americanization Studies of the Carnegie Foundation.

Further, a study of one foreign race among us is also in some part a study of American civilization. It will obviously be fragmentary and without unity; but sidelights and a flash here and there may disclose parts of actual structure that need to be known. These alien races form the human sub-structure of many of our industries. Our treatment of them is one test of the social institutions of our democracy. Do we avail ourselves of the highest scientific knowledge in our treatment of potential citizens? Are the trained psychologists, sociologists, and educators, behind our policies and methods? In a democracy, the problem of the potential citizen must be a major one. If we find that intelligent and trained opinion is not being used in treating one problem, it occasions the query, Are we using more rational methods in other fields? Furthermore, it is interesting to raise the question as to how justly in the eyes of a new group of the foreign-born, our democratic institutions are functioning.

Sociology maintains that if the social point of view which the foreigner brings with him, and the social forces which are to act upon him are known, the attitude which the majority of his nationality will take toward the foreign country to which they come can be predicted. Even a partial description of these forces will help to explain the resulting attitude of the Russian.[11]

[11] The author strongly urges that the section on "The Social Impress of an Autocracy" in the Appendix be read at this point before taking up Chapter II.

CHAPTER II

MIGRATION AND DISTRIBUTION

First Migrations to Alaska and California

THE beginnings of Russian migration to America read like a romance. Over twenty-five years before the United States declared her independence, as early as 1747, Russian colonists, searching for a better climate and a more fertile soil than Siberia afforded, embarked in rude boats built of green lumber and manned by Russian convicts.[1] Many of them went safely across Bering Sea, along the coast of Alaska and made their first center at Kodiak Island. A profitable fur trade with the Alaskan natives developed, and some of the latter were won over to the Russian Orthodox faith. In 1792 the Holy Synod sent out a special mission of monks to minister to the colonists and their converts, and the first Orthodox Church was built in America. It proved successful and thousands of natives were baptized. From that time on until the transfer of Alaska to the United States, the number of Russians steadily increased.

They pushed out in all directions. Some went on

[1] *Cf.* Semple, E. C., *Influences of Geographic Environment* (N. Y., 1911), p. 29.

to Baronoff Island; by 1812 they had explored the California coast, and decided to locate in the redwood belt of Sonoma County. The tract of timber was the deciding factor in the location; with it they fenced their farms, built their homes and even established a ship-building plant. They constructed the first ocean-going vessel launched on this side of the Pacific. For thirty years they grew and prospered. They had their cultivated farms, their herds, their schools and churches.

Unexpectedly one day a ship arrived from Russia; in a few minutes the cannon on the cliff were booming and the bell in the Greek Church was ringing, calling the Russians to assemble. Owing to trouble with Spain, the Tsar's régime had ordered the colonists to return at once. Still believing, as they did, in the Tsar, there was only one thing for them to do. Sorrowfully they abandoned all the accumulations of their toil, and embarked for home. The redwood buildings still stand as monuments to their adventurous achievement.[2]

Later on, after the sale of Alaska in 1867, many more of the Russians returned home, while others went to California. As a result of their influence, the headquarters of the Russian Church in America was removed to San Francisco in 1872. Since that time, California has always contained an important Russian colony.

[2] Gregory, T., *Sonoma County, California*, pp. 18-28; Bancroft, *History of California*, vol. 1, pp. 298, 628-635; vol. 2, chaps. xiv, xxviii.

A Slow Aggregation

It was not until 1872 that from the entire Russian empire, exclusive of Poland, as many as one thousand immigrants entered the United States in any one year.[3] By 1882 the number had increased to 16,918 and in 1892 reached its high water-mark for any year in the nineteenth century, with 81,511 immigrants. These figures, however, are of little value as an indication of the actual number of Russian Slavs who came to America. The records of the census are not sufficiently detailed. Until 1899, with the exception of Poland, all who came from territory controlled by the Tsar's government were classified as Russians. The statistics of those entering from 1899 to 1910 show that the predominating element from the Empire, or 43.8 per cent, were Jews; next came the Poles with 27.0 per cent, while the Russians comprised only 4.4 per cent, the remainder being scattered among various other nationalities.[4] It seems probable, therefore, that up to 1899 the number of Russian Slavs was insignificant. From Russia the Jews were the chief settlers in America and their enthusiastic reports stimulated the Russians themselves to make the venture.

From the year 1899, however, there was almost a steady increase in the number of Russian immigrants until in the year 1913 alone there entered a total of

[3] *Reports of the Immigration Commission* (1911), vol. 3, table 9, p. 14.
[4] *Ibid.*, vol. 3, p. 52.

51,472. In 1914, the war stopped further immigration from Russia and to-day a revolutionary Bolshevik power prohibits emigration, so that from 1914 on, America has been, if anything, losing Russians through emigration instead of gaining them.

Estimated Numbers in America

There were in the United States in 1910, according to the census, 57,926 foreign-born Russians; but 13,781 were Russians from Austria and 1,400 were from Hungary. On the other hand, 3,402 persons were counted as Ruthenians who came out of Russia. In all, therefore, probably about 46,147 foreign-born Russians were to be found in the United States in 1910.[5] In addition, the same census records 37,211 Russians of foreign or mixed parentage born in this country. From July 1, 1910, to June 30, 1919, there has been a net increase of 76,595 Russians over those departing.[6] This would make a total now in the United States of 159,953; but we have not included the surplus of births over deaths among the Russians here. Yet the 1920 Census records 392,049 foreign-born Russians in the

[5] In considering these figures it should be remembered that our census listed as Russians all those who called Russian their native language. But since the last Russian census, in 1897, records the fact that two per cent of the entire European population were Jews who would fall within this class, and since the great majority of emigrants to America from Russia were Jews, undoubtedly much more than two per cent were so included in our census. *Cf.* *Thirteenth Census, Population,* vol. 1, table 3, p. 963.

[6] U. S. Bureau of Immigration, *Annual Report of the Commissioner-General of Immigration.*

United States and including those born in America of Russian parentage, a total of 731,949. Those familiar with the methods of census enumeration know that this number is open to a large possible error. Different authorities make widely varying estimates. The Inter-Racial Council and the President of the Central Executive Committee of the Federation of Russian Organizations in the United States, Professor Alexander Petrunkevich of Yale, estimate that in 1920 there were at least 400,000 Russians here,[7] while Dr. Hourwich, a well-known writer on immigration, places the number below 300,000.[8] The figure given by the Secretary to the Russian Consul General in the same year was approximately half a million, while that of the head of the Russian department of the American Red Cross is as high as 600,000. Although these conjectures are of uncertain value, the official census figures would seem to justify accepting the number as about 700,000, although this is an increase of 700 per cent since 1910.

Distribution

When the Russian first lands in America, he is practically in poverty. From 1910 to 1914 inclusive, out of 155,002 only 8,332, or 5.3 per cent, had over fifty dollars.[9] Almost penniless, his first task

---

[7] *The Standard,* February, 1920, p. 176.
[8] Estimate given in an interview with the writer.
[9] U. S. Bureau of Immigration, *Annual Report of the Commissioner-General of Immigration,* table 7, pp. 20-21, 1910; pp. 20-21, 1911; pp. 74-75, 1912; pp. 46-47, 1913; pp. 42-43, 1914.

is to find employment. His destination is usually
determined by one or both of two factors, the demand for hard labor in factory and mine, and the
location of other Russian groups.

The following table is only indicative of the distribution of the Russians in the United States to-day:

State	The Number of Russians in the Chief States According to the Census of 1910 in the Order of Their Importance		The Intended Future Residence of the Russians Admitted to the United States From 1910 to 1919 [10]	
	Order	Number	Order	Number
New York...............	1	34,612	1	50,189
Pennsylvania	2	24,558	2	27,401
Illinois	3	4,036	4	15,199
New Jersey..............	4	4,031	6	7,861
Ohio	5	3,871	8	4,384
Connecticut	6	3,013	7	7,328
Massachusetts	7	2,674	3	16,372
North Dakota............	8	1,886	20	920
Maryland	9	1,875	9	4,146
California	10	1,828	11	2,997
Minnesota	11	1,517	13	2,453
Michigan	12	1,274	5	8,378
Missouri	13	1,104	17	1,119
Wisconsin	14	956	15	2,029
Washington	15	666	10	3,222
Colorado	16	546	27	490
Iowa	17	511	21	899
Indiana	18	504	16	1,420
West Virginia...........	21	376	14	2,040
New Hampshire..........	29	251	12	2,490
Others	..	5,048	..	9,738
Total		95,137		171,075

According to the distribution in 1910, we find that
of the total, 95,137, New York had over 34,000,

[10] Compiled from the *Annual Reports of the Commissioner-
General of Immigration.*

or 36.5 per cent, Pennsylvania over 24,000 or 25.2
per cent, while New Jersey and Illinois had only
about 4,000 each and Ohio just over 3,800. According to the 1910 Census, five-eighths of all the Russians were in New York and Pennsylvania.

Once a substantial number of Russians have arrived in America and found work, we might expect
that others as they come would seek to join them.
As a matter of fact, we find that those arriving
since the 1910 Census have done this only in part.
At least the table showing the list of the states in
the order of intended future residence of those entering from 1910 until 1919, does not follow exactly the order of the distribution by states as shown
by the Census of 1910.[11] Massachusetts occupies
the seventh instead of the third place, displacing
Illinois. Michigan is in the fifth instead of the
twelfth place, displacing Ohio, Connecticut, and
New Jersey; New Hampshire appears in the twelfth
place instead of the twenty-ninth, while North Dakota falls from eighth to twentieth. These differences seem to reflect changes in our industrial order
and a shifting of nationalities in certain industries.
Massachusetts is now using large numbers of Russians in her textile industries which have expanded
rapidly since 1910. Michigan has developed huge

[11] It must be remembered that this is not necessarily conclusive
evidence. Each table is based on different data, one representing
where the Russians actually were in 1910, the other where, since
that date, the Russians declared they were going to live after their
entry into the United States.

automobile plants, while New Hampshire now uses large numbers of Russians in her paper mills.   As for North Dakota, she has little more available good land for homesteading and, in any case, a large amount of capital is needed to develop it successfully.

No doubt the war played its part in shifting the Russians to the munition and shipbuilding centers. New England now has a larger number of Russians than it had in 1910.   The Inter-Racial Council estimated in 1920 the approximate numbers of Russians in the more important states as follows: "New York, 60,000; Illinois, 50,000; Massachusetts, 40,-000; Pennsylvania, 35,000; Ohio, 45,000; Michigan, 30,000; New Jersey, 35,000; Connecticut, 20,-000.   According to the same source the largest Russian colonies are to be found in the following cities: New York, 25,000; Detroit, 17,000; Chicago, 20,-000; San Francisco, 15,000; Pittsburgh, 14,000; Philadelphia, 12,000; Newark, 10,000; Jersey City, 8,000; Cleveland, 5,000; St. Louis, 5,000." [12]

Migration Within the United States

Within the United States, the Russian family groups do not move often.   After talking with over one hundred families scattered in the various cities visited, the writer found that eighty-five per cent of them, irrespective of the length of their stay in

[12] Vilchur, M., *The Russians in America* (N. Y., 1918), gives approximately the same figures, pp. 60-61.

the United States, had not made more than one change from city to city, if they had moved at all. This is, of course, not a large enough statistical sample to be conclusive, but it seems probable, once a family is settled, takes in boarders, rents a house or apartment, that it would find moving difficult, and the testimony of the Russian priests to the author was one further confirmatory evidence. It is chiefly during strike conditions, general unemployment, or unusual opportunities to secure better work, that the Russian family moves. If the man hears of better work elsewhere, he will sometimes go alone to test it out, sending for the family if everything proves satisfactory.

Russians without families in this country move somewhat more frequently. Some of them have been in as many as eight different states in five years, but this is unusual. In seventy-eight cases of Russian political prisoners in Detroit who came to the United States within the last fourteen years,[13] the following facts are significant: twelve out of the 78 or 15 per cent had remained in the same place since coming to America, the average number of changes in residence was 2.2 times in 7 years.[14] These facts seem to indicate that even the single Russians do not move often. These men may not have been typical of the average Russian, but it would appear that those who have been arrested or who

---

[13] Only two of these had wives in this country.
[14] From a personal investigation made by the author.

have grown dissatisfied through failure to become adjusted to America, would move more frequently than those who have become so adjusted.

Summary

The aggregation of Russians in the United States has conformed to a law both of physics and of sociology: it has followed the line of least resistance. The mass of Russians have taken the first positions that were available and this has concentrated them in urban communities. According to the United States Census, 87 per cent of all the foreign-born from the Russian empire exclusive of Finland lived there in 1910.[15] Because they have been played upon in like ways by similar forces they have become segregated in colonies and industrial centers. The various social and economic forces in Russia and America have acted on them to place them where they were just as truly as have the giant glaciers acted on certain boulders and rocks to leave them in the valleys. In the succeeding chapters we shall attempt to trace other forces which are molding the attitude of these newcomers towards our people and our country.

[15] *Thirteenth Census, Population,* vol. 1, table 22, p. 818.

CHAPTER III

WE have seen that the economic and social conditions of the Russian newcomers force them to accept almost any opening in the labor market. We shall now attempt to analyze some of the definite stimuli which affect them in their new and strange economic world.

Means of Livelihood

The Russian born are chiefly to be found among the lowest types of manual laborers in the mines and factories of America. Definite statistics as to what proportions are engaged in the various occupations at the present time are not obtainable. The United States Immigration Commission made a study in 1909 of 507,256 wage-earners in mines and manufacturing establishments of America and found that of these, 1.6 per cent of the male and .9 per cent of the female foreign-born workers were Russian. To be more exact, there were 6,588 male and 914 female foreign-born Russian workers and 1,299 male and 1,305 female native-born workers of Russian parents constituting in all 1.5 per cent of the total number of wage-earners investigated. Most of the foreign-born were found in coal mining and in the iron and steel industries. This fact has been confirmed by other studies.[1] A ranking of the industries according to the number found employed in them made by the Immigration Commission follows:

Industry	Russian Parentage Born in Russia	Born in U. S.
Coal Mining	1,853	176
Iron and Steel	1,372	150
Slaughtering, Meat Packing	1,010	324
Clothing	536	555
Wool and Worsted Goods	527	52
Cotton Goods	471	87
Sugar Refining	372	21
Agricultural Implements	307	250
Cigars and Tobacco	220	180
Leather	207	106
Glass	147	84
Boots and Shoes	123	64
Oil Refining	103	14
Construction Work	103	2
Silk Goods	70	489
Iron, Ore Mining	24	6
Collars, Cuffs and Shirts	22	4
Furniture	18	21
Copper Mining, Smelting	6	17
Silk Dyeing	5	0

These statistics record over three times as many foreign as native born. They seem to indicate that the second generation Russian leaves the harder lines of work and shifts into the easier. For example, in coal mining there was the proportion of 10 foreign to one native-born of Russian parents, in iron and steel 9 to 1, and in sugar refining about

[1] Vilchur, M., *The Russians in America, op. cit.,* p. 62; Balch, E. G., *Our Slavic Fellow Citizens* (N. Y., 1910), p. 282.

18 to 1. Yet in agricultural implements, leather, glass, boots and shoes, and tobacco there are over half as many native of Russian parents as foreignborn; in clothing there are more of the second generation, while in silk goods there are seven times as many.[2]

Another investigation conducted by the U. S. Immigration Commission in 1909 among 80,000 employees on the Pacific Coast and in the Rocky Mountain States showed that the greatest number of Russians were in the following industries, in the order of their importance:[3] 1, steam railway; 2, coal mining; 3, lumber; 4, beet sugar manufacturing; 5, canneries; 6, glass; 7, smelting; 8, cement; 9, electric railways. It will be noticed that these are all industries in which large numbers of unskilled workers are employed. The Russians take the job at the bottom of the ladder; they have the roughest and hardest tasks; as they express it in their native language, they do the "black work." This is doubtless inevitable since they are illiterate, penniless, and speak a foreign language, but it is unfortunate that the conditions in the industries employing these marginal workers should be as unfavorable as they are.

[2] It should also be borne in mind that the Russian immigration is new, and that these industries may use more children than the others.

[3] *Abstracts of Reports of the Immigration Commission,* vol. 1, table 3, p. 627.

Conditions of Labor

We have seen that the greatest number of Russians are found in coal mining and the iron and steel industry. Let us examine briefly the conditions under which they labor. Judge Gary has admitted that 69,000 men have been working the twelve-hour day (that is from eleven to fourteen hours) for the U. S. Steel Corporation.[4] The author's investigation as well as that of others including the Inter-Church and the Pittsburgh Survey, has found that most of the Russians are in the class that has been working in this way; they are subjected not only to the twelve-hour shift but the seven-day week.[5] About every fortnight they have been forced to work an eighteen- or twenty-four-hour day, when the turn from a night to a day shift occurred. "In some plants the thirty-six-hour turn is still not unknown." [6] What this means in the actual life of the employee can be realized by the testimony of one of them. "Time on the job, 91 hours; eating, about 9; street car (45 minutes each way), 10.5; sleep (7½ hours a day), 52.5; dressing, undressing, washing, and so forth, 5; that totals 168 or every single hour in the week, and it's how I slave." This is not a rare occurrence for those who live a

---

[4] U. S. Senate Committee on Education and Labor, *Investigation of Strike in Steel Industries* (1919), vol. 1, p. 157.
[5] *Inter-Church World Movement Report on the Steel Strike of 1919* (N. Y., 1920), pp. 44-84.
[6] *Ibid.*, p. 47.

considerable distance from their work, and is bitterly resented. As another Slavic worker expressed it, "Wor'rk, wor'rk always every day, every week, ten hours days and twelve hours nights—alla time— no spell—and alla time every d—— furnace hongry." [7] The twelve-hour day does violence to the Russian's play instinct just as truly as to that of an American, although each might find expression for it in a different manner. Furthermore, as the Inter-Church report says, "The twelve-hour day makes any attempt at 'Americanization' or other civic or individual development for one-half of all immigrant steel workers arithmetically impossible." (p. 12).

It is not the long hours alone which arouse resentment, but the fact that in contrast to former work in the fields, the present tasks are hazardous, unhealthful and unpleasant. To those who have been through a large steel mill at night a description is unnecessary. For those who have not, let me quote from an officer of a steel company who himself went into the steel mills and worked as a common laborer for several months during 1919: "Then when the white-hot steel is roaring and blazing into the huge ladle—he must lift large paper sacks of coal to his shoulder, run towards the ladle and with all his strength hurl them into the blazing, scorching torrent. Thereupon the flames, fed by the

---

[7] Williams, W., *What's on the Worker's Mind* (N. Y., 1920), p. 25.

carbon, leap to the roof and the heat is fearful." [8]
Or again the same observer remarked that he could
not have stayed ten minutes in the checker chamber: the temperature was so high that scientists
could prove it was impossible to maintain life there
(*sic*). Yet the foreigners endure it for half-hour
periods at a time, taking out brick.[9] The reaction
of a Russian to these tasks, while not so violent as
that of an American, nevertheless is distinct. Even
when the tasks are not so hazardous as the ones
mentioned, they are likely to be grindingly monotonous and are carried on at a higher speed and more
continuously than anything the Russian has before
known.

In the mines the hours are shorter, but the
lack of light and air and the constant stooping position (depending on the mine worked) is just as
strange. Furthermore, the Russian claims that he
is assigned the worst seams where the work is hardest and the proportion of slag is greatest. In general, the conditions of labor in the mines have been
found better than in steel.[10] Nevertheless, many
Russians, owing to the irregularity of the employment and the underground work, prefer the steel
industry.[11]

[8] *Ibid.*, p. 35.
[9] *Ibid.*, p. 247.
[10] *Cf.* Commons, J. R., in *Charities and Commons* (1909), XXI,
p. 1051.
[11] From 1913-18 the average number of forced idle days in the
coal areas of Illinois, Indiana, Ohio, and Pittsburgh was over 158.
Stelzle, C., *World Outlook*, Jan., 1920, p. 38.

For the larger proportion of Russians, the job is their first real taste of America and it is decidedly a bitter one. The contrast to Russia makes it difficult for him successfully to adjust himself to the speed and monotony of large scale production even in such employments as textile or automobile manufacture. Nevertheless, those who find themselves in mining or steel might change to other industries if they knew how, but the difficulties in the way appear formidable. In ordinary times it is no easy task to find work in an unfamiliar occupation. Unless the immigrant were particularly fortunate after his arrival, he must have had an anxious period of hunting employment. The fear of joblessness and of the loss of savings makes him endure what he otherwise would not. Even in such a prosperous year as 1919, Whiting Williams, a college graduate with a splendid physique, had great difficulty in getting work.[12] How much harder it must have been for the Russian is indicated by the fact that hundreds were out of employment in Pittsburgh alone in the same year.[13]

The Employer

In the early stages of American industry the Russian might have hoped at least to see his employer. There would have been a chance for some point of

---

[12] Williams, *op. cit.*, pp. 3-10.
[13] According to testimony given to the writer by representatives of the International Institute, by the Russians themselves, and by investigators of the Inter-Church World Movement.

contact making for mutual understanding and co-operation. To-day except for vague concepts from hearsay and misrepresentation, the employer is an entirely unknown quantity to the Russian. Nor is this entirely one-sided. In the "absentee" type of corporation to which the basic industries of which we have been speaking belong, the employer rarely sees, much less knows, anything about the workmen. This is well illustrated in the steel industry. As the Inter-Church report states, "Ultimate control of the plants was vested in a small group of financiers whose relation to the producing force was remote. The financial group's machinery of control gave it full knowledge of output and dividends but negligible information of working and living conditions." [14]

In the investigation conducted by the writer in factories and mines in Eastern states, the management seemed to know almost nothing about the Russians employed. In many cases they did not even know how many of that nationality were on their books, for Poles, Finns, Jews and other races were lumped together. At one time the sending out of a questionnaire to manufacturers on the number of Russians employed, their health, housing and living conditions, was considered by the writer. The project was abandoned on the advice of the personnel departments of a number of plants, who said the companies themselves did not have the facts.

[14] Inter-Church Report, *op. cit.*, p. 11.

The personnel superintendent of the Winchester Repeating Arms Co., for example, said that although that company has been employing Russians in all departments, they have "no statistics to show how many there are." A letter from the secretary to the Immigration Committee of the Merchants and Manufacturers Association of New York City, advised that such a questionnaire would be useless, as "most large employers know very little about the character or habits of their employees aside from productive ability." [15]

The attitude which an employer assumes towards the worker is partly the product of social pressure and in some cases seems to have its primary source in the organs of public opinion. At any rate, after the scare about the Bolsheviks had been sensationally exploited by our press, Russians began to be laid off right and left simply on account of their nationality. Harvey Anderson, formerly in charge of Y.M.C.A. work for Russians in America, sums up the general situation in 1919 as follows: "Since the 'Bolshevik' régime began in Russia, the Russian is regarded everywhere as a 'Bolshevik' and is shunned. I encountered a case the other day where an employer got the idea that the distinguishing feature of a 'Bolshevik' was a beard, so he refused to give employment to some faithful and loyal Old Believers whose religious conviction does not permit them to shave. Whenever the employer has

[15] Letter to the writer from M. E. Dodge, Dec. 29, 1920.

found it necessary to cut down the number of employees, the Russian has been the first to go. When he seeks new employment he is inevitably met with the suspicion that he is a 'Bolshevik' and he goes on hunting for a job and in his soul grows and grows a spirit of revolt. He begins to hate America and everything American, and is ready to believe anything bad about her." [16]

The inevitable result has been that whereas these men were good honest workers, they became revolters against the existing order. This is expressed in a letter from an educated Russian of Worcester, Mass.: "Many thousands of Russians in this country while they work have hardly enough to live on, and now that the war is ended, they are discharged from factories, and told 'You are a Bolshevik.' Many of them do not know what Bolshevism and what capitalism mean—but they make real Bolsheviks out of them." In Akron in 1920 some Russians even shaved their beards and used English names in order to get jobs as Americans.

Representatives of several large firms frankly told the writer that they refused employment to Russians. "We can get plenty of other nationalities," said one employer, "why take Bolsheviks?" Unfortunately, from the standpoint of the Russian worker, it does not seem quite so simple or so fair. He comes to our country, works seven years in the steel plant, loses his best strength in the work, and

[16] From an unpublished statement transmitted to the author.

then is laid off because the Bolsheviks seize control in Russia. The great majority stoically struggle on, but a priest told me of two who were found dead on the railroad track with the following note in Russian: "We prefer death to starvation. Have slaved in a steel plant for seven years. Now they discharge us and we can't find a job."

This discrimination against the Russian on the part of the employer, and lack of information, lead to equally absurd conclusions by the worker, who is led to believe that like the rich barons in Russia, the greedy capitalist is exploiting him for profit. Mr. Whiting Williams, whom we have mentioned, after his experience as a laborer, states that "the relation between the large employer and, for the most part, the foreign-born and foreign-speaking worker in the labor gangs" is expressed by the phrase of the workers, "Aw, w'at da hell! w'at da hell da companee care 'bout us?" Mr. Williams concludes that the astounding ignorance of the worker "concerning the plans and purposes, the aims and ideals, the character of the other human element in the same problem, his employer, is unequaled by anything I can think of—unless it is his employer's ignorance of him! To each the other stands as the 'x' in the equation of the factory organization." [17]

Because this is true, it is all the more unfortunate and a potential cause of trouble that there is no

[17] Williams, W., *Collier's Weekly,* July 3, 1920, p. 7.

department in a great many of these plants to settle a grievance or to give information.   Mistakes occur in industrial life as elsewhere, and too often the Slav does not know how to secure redress.   Even Mr. Williams found himself "fired" when he tried to secure a loan on the wages already due him in a steel plant.   In another case he nearly lost his wages because he had no time card and on leaving the company was unable to secure his money because it was not pay day.[18]   These and a hundred other things occur with Russian workers who do not know English and, not having the social background to understand that it is partly their own fault, they often set it down as deliberate injustice.

Accidents

The feeling that the employer, like the Russian baron, cares nothing for the worker, receives a further stimulus from the prevalence of accidents and the absence, in many cases, of any particular effort on the part of the company to make permanent provision for the injured.   Although the employers' liability laws and safety appliances have eliminated both a great many accidents and also a large share of the injustice connected with them, there is still room for a great deal of improvement.   In the coal mines alone there were 2,317 fatalities in 1919 and 2,260 in 1920.[19]   Indeed the average death rate

[18] Williams, W., *op. cit.*, pp. 144 and 161.
[19] U. S. Bureau of Mines, *Monthly Statement of Coal Mine Fatalities in the United States,* June, 1921, p. 6.

from accidents in coal mining per one thousand workers in the United States is three times that of Great Britain.[20] The number of those who are merely injured in coal mining and in the iron and steel industry, although unknown must be far larger. Yet a surprising number of injured Russians still claim never to have received any compensation. In the few cases the author attempted to investigate, the failure seemed to be due to the ignorance of the Russian, his lack of legal advice, and the fact that he feared that action on his part might debar him from all chances of further employment by the same company. It also seems to be true that the Russian is indifferent to danger; he is willing to accept hazardous work and therefore is injured oftener than many other nationalities. Nevertheless, in common with most people, after he has been injured, he feels that he has been unfairly treated and is sometimes very bitter about the indifference of the company to his plight. This feeling seems to be shared to some extent by all the Russians.

Most of the states have fairly adequate compensation laws but New Hampshire and New Jersey, two states in which considerable numbers of Russians are employed, still expressly exclude alien non-resident dependents from compensation.[21] Even in Pennsylvania and in New York, the Russians claim

---

[20] *International Labor Review,* vol. v, no. i, Jan., 1922, p. 140.
[21] Pamphlet of the American Association for Labor Legislation, Nov., 1920.

that since communication with Russia has been sev-
ered following the Bolshevik control, no compensation could be collected in most cases for wives and
children in the homeland. The writer has listened
to scores of cases cited by Russian priests, who were
willing to swear to the facts, that injured men of
their congregations had received no compensation
in spite of the law. They, too, testify that the Russian is ignorant of its provisions and has scant legal
aid. The following is merely one illustration from
Father Kozuboff of Hartford: "In the hospital now
there lies a man whose legs were crushed when a
bucket for loading coal broke loose from the chain.
The doctor says he can never walk, yet when he
leaves the hospital he gets nothing, for he has no
witnesses to the accident." Whether or not such
statements are exaggerated, they go to show that the
Russian is a mere cog in the machine of production.
Indeed, he does not receive the care that parts of a
machine do. They are constantly oiled and pro-
tected. Every possible care is taken of them, and
when the machine is not in use a guard is kept on the
premises. But for the human cog, little thought is
taken. He can over-work, eat bad food, sleep in
rooms ill-ventilated and unsanitary—and the employer seemingly cares nothing. When the Russian
"lays off" the job there is too often no human guard
from the factory to see what can be done to help and
protect him. If the cog is smashed to atoms or even
only injured so that he needs patching, the accident

insurance covers the costs. The cog can be replaced immediately without cost by a new Russian. If the machine is broken, it means delay in production and new costs. In a large steel plant visited in the summer of 1920, the doctor stated that an average of one-fifth of the working force visited the dispensary every month. "Most of them come from accidents to their eyes. We have not yet secured glasses which can be worn in the intense heat of the blast furnace," said he.

Now although the Russian is of a stoical temperament and accepts these conditions with seeming indifference, if one can win his confidence, his real thoughts can be uncovered. He feels that he is being treated as a mere tool; that his unknown company employer does not care what happens to him.

The Boss

In contrast to the employer whom he rarely if ever sees, the worker is in very close and constant relations with one man, the boss or foreman, who comes more and more to represent the industry to him. Often he is even hired or fired by the boss and if he does pass through an employment department it is merely for a formal question or two and for registration on the company's books. Not only is the boss an ever-present reality, but he is usually so unlike the Russian that mutual misunderstanding results.

In the great majority of factories and shops which

the writer has visited, the foreman for the unskilled alien is also a foreigner. There were German, Polish, Italian, Irish, Magyar, and Welsh bosses— Mr. Williams speaks also of Greek and Spanish. Too often the most conspicuous "Americanism" they have absorbed is profanity. Mr. Williams expresses it in these words, "The gang bosses, at least those of the labor gangs, seem to be the worst examples of what-the-hell philosophy." [22]   That neither the boss nor the Russian wholly understands the other is but natural, for they are unlike products of different European backgrounds, possessing strong racial antagonisms. Sometimes all they have in common in the matter of language is a most meager vocabulary, slang English, "job" phrases pronounced with a foreign accent to the accompaniment of much profanity. It is natural that when the worker is new, his lack of understanding is profound, hence the number of oaths that are hurled at him is enormous. It is small wonder that he dislikes the boss even when he is an American. H. W. Anderson, formerly in charge of the Y.M.C.A. work for Russians in America, says:

The Russian has ever thought of the government as an oppressor, and he transfers his mistrust, suspicion and hate for the Russian government to the "boss" where he works, who represents to him America. A few days ago we witnessed a typical incident. Something had gone wrong with the work of some Russians. The men were not to blame,

[22] Williams, *op. cit.,* p. 18.

yet the young American foreman blamed it all on the ——,
——, lazy ——. They faced the angry tirade of the foreman with stolid, sullen faces and made no reply, but in their
hearts they registered one more case against America.[23]

This is but a typical specimen of conditions which
are all too widely prevalent.

It is true that some of the Russians draw a dis-
tinction between the squad foreman who works with
them and the boss foreman. The former shares in
their labor and is often friendly, but they consider
the latter as almost invariably bad, feeling that he
deliberately makes them do work that is too difficult.
For example, a Russian in Philadelphia said,
"The boss makes two of us carry steel which should
require four. If I refuse, I lose my job. Lots of
weeks the work is so heavy I get pains in my back
and have to lay off three days out of seven." Or
again, in a mill in Pittsburgh, the boss, Pete, according to the testimony of a Russian, is a giant who
can do the work of two ordinary men. In somewhat exaggerated language more clearly to convey
his meaning, he said: "The boss can lift two tons
himself. He will watch us straining to lift a two-
ton iron and will laugh at us and yell, 'You ——
—— Polack, push.' We will break our backs trying and he will not lift a finger to help us."

Occasionally the writer ran across Russians who
did have good foremen as in the following case.
"Bopp, our foreman, has lost an eye, and is a good

American. When the work is heavy he will help
us. He rarely swears at us, all the other bosses do."
But even in this case, the Russian did not have any
more friendly attitude toward the management. He
seemed to feel that "Bopp" was good in spite of a
grasping and dishonest company.

The Inter-Church Report summarizes what it
considers the grievances in the life of the Russian
immigrant steel worker as follows:

Nine times out of ten he is a peasant, taking an industrial
job for the first time. At the start, only as wages fail to
keep him and his family as he wants them to be kept, or the
hours break down his health, does he care much about "controlling" either wages or hours. What matters most to
him is that if the mill is shut down, he is the first to be laid
off; if the job is unusually hot, greasy, or heavy, he is the
first to be set to it. He is the most arbitrarily, often
brutally, shifted and ordered about; if he takes a lay-off,
he is the most likely to be heavily docked, and he is the
most likely to be kept beyond his hour with no additional
pay. If there is sickness in his home or he is otherwise kept
away, his excuses get the shortest shrift. If he is the butt
of unusual prejudice in either his foreman or some fellow
worker evinced in profanity or the penalties of always the
nastier task, he knows least where to go for redress or how
to speak it.[24]

Yet the writer is convinced that aside from the
fact that the Russian is usually the marginal worker,

[24] Inter-Church Report, *op. cit.*, pp. 135-136. The above quotation includes certain other foreign workers besides the Russian.)

most of these grievances arise directly from his relations with the boss who to the worker typifies the industry.

For his Master's thesis at Chicago University, J. S. Cole [25] made a careful study of 112 single Russians, the majority of whom were either employed in the stock yards of Chicago or in stables, or were temporarily out of work. He reported that they were very bitter against the boss, their attitude being summed up in the following remarks:

"Before war, very good; but now all, no matter what nationality, laid off on least excuse. If horse no can pull wagon, put on another horse. If man no can pull truck, lay him off."

"Foreman very severe; sometimes lay off day for being minute late. Rush so at work that you almost faint. Treatment worse now since it is very easy to replace men."

"Boss very hard. Fired one man, he was in his place two minutes before whistle blew to enter shop."

"Bosses very unreasonable. One man left truck to get drink and boss fired him. Have to bribe boss to keep job."

"Too strict about time; if one minute late, dock one-half hour. Getting worse all the time. Often work so hard get weak and when tell foreman he says we are drunk."

[25] Cole, J. S. R. (Chicago, 1919), unpublished study transmitted to the author.

"Treat Russian like dog."

After talking with several hundred Russians in mining and steel plants, the writer found the responses much the same; ninety per cent or more fear and hate the boss. Even when ignorant of English they are all familiar with the common epithet he hurls at them, "You —— —— Polack." The disregard of all racial distinctions simply accentuates the insult. In their eyes the boss is as autocratic and domineering as the Tsar's officials. And so, during working hours, the chief social bond affecting the worker's effort is despotic power and a fear-inspired obedience. This is not true of all the Russian workers, but there is something of this feeling among a great many. It is tempered by the fact that they are free to leave the employment permanently at the end of a day's work, but in that case the job is gone and savings begin to dwindle. The Russians expressed their feelings to the writer in these terms—to cite two examples:

"The boss is worse than the Tsar's officials; they would flog us and let us go, he drives us to a slow death."

"If he were good, would not be boss. Boss like dog, always snapping and swearing at everybody."

These reactions in the mind of the Russian show how little friendship he has for the boss. No doubt part of this is inevitable in the relationship which must exist between the one directing a task and a group of ignorant foreigners who are doing the actual disagreeable work, yet at present it does seem that the relationship is unnecessarily antagonistic. Apparently little or no attempt is made in our basic industries to give adequate instruction to the foremen or bosses in the art of human relations, and as a result the Russian does not see the good side of the management or of America in the factory or mine. Instead, the contrast to his former free peasant toil in the fields eats into his soul; the boss has instilled the caustic of resentment. He is the taskmaster who drives him on at a killing pace, who exploits him—he seems to represent America.

The Labor Union

The Russian toiling at the bottom of our industrial ladder has no chance to join the ordinary trade union which is jealously watched over by the skilled or semi-skilled. Even for the exceptional Russian of ability, the initiation fee is likely to be higher than he cares to pay. One of the educated Russians, a skillful carpenter, told me he could not afford to pay the initiation fee, nor did he care to serve as an apprentice at the low rate of pay required by the Union before he would be eligible for the better position. He preferred to work as a non-union man.

For the rank and file of the Russians working outside of the mines, there is little opportunity to join a labor group other than the I.W.W., or the purely Russian political organization known as "The

Union of Russian Workers," which will be treated in another chapter. The head of the Union's Federation in Akron stated that although there were hundreds of Russians in the rubber plants, there was not a single one in the Union.

On the other hand, as we have already noted, the Russian in his native land has been used to coöperation. He is therefore willing and eager to join with his fellows in a class organization. Furthermore, in industrial conflicts his idealism and loyalty to the union even at great cost to himself are well known. No doubt the most important reason for this is that he feels the bad conditions under which he is working and that he has less to lose, but there is still another reason: he is used to hardship and coöperative effort and will endure to the end if the group will thereby gain. This was shown in the great anthracite coal strike of 1902, in the strike in the Chicago slaughter houses in 1904, in the textile strike in Massachusetts and the steel strike in Pennsylvania in 1919.[26] The attitude of the Russians in the steel industry as an American labor organizer, W. Z. Foster, views it, follows:

He has that group idea very strongly developed. In his own country individualism plays a small part. He is labeled and tagged and oppressed, and he is classed, and his psychology is pretty simple over there. He knows what he is, and if there is any possible chance for him to do anything, he feels that it is as a group, not as an individual.

[26] *Cf.* Balch, *op. cit.,* pp. 290-291.

He comes over here and he seems to respond to an appeal better than Americans do. But he is very materialistic in his demands. You know you can convince the Americans and you can hold an organization for years in a plant without getting a cent of benefit out of it directly. But the foreigner you can't hold that way. He comes in for increase of wages and shortening of hours. He comes in quite readily, but if you don't get him the results, he drops away quite readily also.

Then a peculiar thing happens. When the fight occurs, he is a splendid fighter. He has the American beaten when it comes to a fight. I don't say that in criticism of the American, but I think it is due to the position he occupies in the industry. The American usually holds the good job, and he has a home half paid for, and he is full of responsibility; whereas the foreigner is more foot-loose; has a poor job anyway, and he doesn't feel that so much is at stake.

He will stick, while the American will go back to work. That is what happened in the mills just now. When the fight occurs the foreigner displays a wonderful amount of idealism, a wonderful amount of stick-to-it-iveness that is altogether dissimilar to the intensely materialistic spirit he shows in his union transactions.[27]

The Bulletins issued every few days by the National Committee for Organizing Iron and Steel Workers were printed in Slavic and Polish as well as English. The Russian workers usually had some one who could read either one of these languages or could translate from the English. The character of the text was naturally not such as to make them

[27] Inter-Church Report, *op. cit.,* pp. 162-163.

look favorably on our capitalists or the American press. Several of the Russian workers furnished copies and the following is from Number 13, dated October 23, 1919:

"Trade Unions are mighty in power, but their power is not like the power of the Steel Trust. The Steel Trust has millions and millions of dollars to fight with; the labor unions have no money or very little, but they have millions and millions of men."

Bulletin Number 12, dated October 20, states that the Homestead steel plant, in absolute contradiction to the newspaper accounts, is closed instead of "running 'practically' at capacity."

These bulletins, together with inflammatory speeches at those meetings which were permitted, as well as the action of the constabulary, to be treated later, increased the hostility of the Russians towards America. When the strike was lost, the Russians complained about the Union as useless and of American workers as traitors for going back before it was ended. "We didn't start the strike," said one to me, "Americans are at the head of it. They told us that we would be traitors to our fellow workmen if we did not support it. Now we have done it and the newspapers call us 'reds,' 'I.W.W.'s,' 'Bolsheviks.' Us they refuse to take back, but the Americans get their jobs."

One of these men whom the writer visited was refused employment following the strike. It so happened that his tenement house was right next to the steel plant. After two months' search he found a job in a mill one hour away by street car. He worked eleven hours a day one week and thirteen hours a night the next. On his night shift fifteen hours were spent daily at his work and traveling to and fro. It is small wonder that he was bitterly discouraged and blamed the union and America. His wife claimed that they went to church when they could, and before they had become disillusioned by the heartlessness of the corporation they had believed in America. An American flag and a religious picture over the bed seemed to confirm her statement. She concluded, "We now know America means money. We Russians are only like flies, too small—company doesn't care."

The United Mine Workers of America is one of the few industrial unions accepting all who work in and about the mines for membership. Consequently, nearly all the Russians engaged in the coal industry belong to it, although their exact membership is not known, all Slavs being classed together. According to the union officials, the Russians make very faithful members. The weekly journal of the Union contains three pages in Slovak. While, as many writers claim, the unions do a great deal toward Americanizing the foreigner,[28] it is not strange that they should represent the coal corporations in a bad light. The United Mine Workers oppose I. W. W.-

---

[28] Balch, *op. cit.*, p. 292, and article by Charles Stelzle, *World Outlook*, Jan., 1920, p. 27.

ism, Bolshevism, and radicalism, but they do not hesitate to acquaint their members with what they consider unjust in our industrial order. For example, one number of their journal [29] has articles entitled "Harrowing Story of Fiendish Cruelty Practiced on Families of Non-Union Miners at Crucible, Pa.," "Cruel Discrimination by Harlan County Operators," "If a Coal Miner Is Guilty, Is an Operator Guilty for Doing the Very Same Thing?" "More Misrepresentation," "More of That Propaganda." These articles attack the corporations and statements of such men as Judge Gary and Senator Pomerene of Ohio. On the other hand, the same number says much about the honesty of the American people as a whole and proclaims the fact that the miners "believe in and uphold American ideals." In spite of this the United Mine Workers of America are not making the Russians enthusiastic supporters of our nation, they see too much of the dark side. Moreover, they do not often mingle with the American men. As several of the Russian and Slavic organizers, interviewed, said: "The Russians are loyal to the Union. They pay their dues well, but they stick together and take little interest in the meetings which are usually run by Americans or leaders of other nationalities. We are content if they pay their dues." If this is true even in the United Mine Workers organization, to which a great many of the Russians belong, it can

[29] Jan. 15, 1920 (appeared during a strike period).

readily be understood that, taken as a whole, the social impress of the Union on the Russian is not great. He accepts it where he has the chance, but it does not vitally concern him; he is an outsider, a passive participant in its activities. His relation to the Union at least teaches him something of democratic government, for he has an equal vote with his American fellow workers even though he otherwise plays a minor part.

Wages

As would be expected with a marginal worker, the Russian is receiving a low rate of pay. Judge Gary admits that 70,000 men in the steel industry are receiving the lowest rate.[30] We have already indicated that the Russians are in this class. The rate of pay was "less than enough for the average American family's subsistence," [31] according to the budgets of Professor Ogburn, Professor Chapin, the New York Factory Commission, the New York Board of Estimate, all brought up to date to conform to the rise in the cost of living.[32] But in the matter of money wages, the Russian is vastly better off than he was in his home land, and this is one of the big compensations to him for the hard conditions. If he can but save enough, some day he will return to Russia as a comparatively wealthy peas-

[30] Inter-Church Report, *op. cit.,* p. 5.
[31] It must be remembered that the majority of Russians were single or without their wives in America.
[32] *Ibid.,* pp. 225-263, 92-95.

ant. If that is not his ambition, he is able to send amounts, which will seem fabulous to them, back to his relatives or he can send for his wife and children to join him here.

The study of the Immigration Commission in 1909 [33] showed that 2,819 foreign-born Russians received an average wage of $2.06 a day; this was three cents below the average of all the foreign-born. The 248 of the second generation received only an average of $1.98, which was 35 cents below the general average of native-born of foreign fathers. This may be partially explained on the supposition that the children of the Russians are younger because Russian immigration is newer.

The war increased wages tremendously; the ordinary day laborer who had been getting two to three dollars a day (in Bridgeport, Youngstown, Cleveland and other centers) during the war reached as high as forty or more cents an hour. By means of a large output and overtime rates some of the men received as high as fifty dollars a week. But after the war the earnings of Russians began to drop again. A study of 95 single Russians in Chicago in 1919 revealed the fact that they were making from 12 to 30 dollars a week. The overwhelming majority and the average number earned 23 dollars. Of 112 Russians studied in this same report, 10, or 9.4 per cent, were out of employment and had been so from three weeks to four months.

[33] Abstract, vol. 1, table 26, *op. cit.,* p. 371.

They claimed discrimination on account of their nationality.[34] In Pittsburgh in 1920 the writer found that the average Russian workman received from $25-30 a week, but this does not take into account time lost from shutdown, sickness and other causes. In the next chapter we shall discuss the standard of living which the Russian maintains. The amount he saves, however, because of his frugality and thrift is at least a partial indication of whether his pay is more than enough to meet the standards he is willing to endure.

No matter how much the Russians were earning, we know that a good many were saving money. From July 1, 1913 to June 30, 1914, 546,775 postal money orders totaling $13,469,839.02 were sent to Russia or an average of about $24.60 per order.[35] Because of the outbreak of the war, the amount in subsequent years was not significant. The statistics of the money sent through the Russian Consul General in New York are:

	For Deposit	For Friends	Total	Average Remittance for the Two Years
1916	$359,711.55	$ 38,311.76	$ 395,023.31	$151
1917	776,265.48	283,993.95	1,060,259.43	

But since some send twice in the year, the consul believes that the yearly average per person making remittances in 1916 was much more and in 1917, nearly double. The Russian Embassy undertook an

[34] Cole, unpublished study, *cf. supra,* p. 34.
[35] U. S. Post Office Dept., *Annual Reports, 1914,* p. 360.

investigation of the financial condition of the Russians in America in November, 1918 under the direction of Professor C. V. Gayman who visited the various colonies and secured first-hand information from Russian individuals and banks. His report though never published contains financial estimates of value. He found that the average amount of money per individual sent to Russia yearly through private banks was $250. Now of course these figures include the Jews who are more prosperous than the average Russian laborer. Moreover, Mr. Gayman believes that they represent only one quarter of the total Russian group. Even so, they indicate a probability that the other Russians were also saving.

At the second general (*Syezd*) meeting of Russian organizations held in New York City on the 13th of December, 1918, eighty of the two hundred or more delegates had an average of $900 in the bank. The others did not give the amount of their savings. Of course all the delegates represented some organization and were presumably above the average Russian working man. Mr. Gayman estimates that Russians without families are able to deposit $250 each year. Mr. Vilchur states that in 1917 the average Russian was saving from 20-25 dollars a month; [36] but since the war this has been greatly reduced. Mr. Cole in his Chicago report found that out of 112 Russians, all of whom had

[36] Vilchur, M., *The Russians in America, op. cit.*, p. 68 .

been saving before the war, only twenty were able to do so in 1919. In traveling among the Russian colonies, the writer found conditions varying in this respect, but in general, most of the single Russians save something. All claim that it is much less than before the war. This is in large measure due to higher standards of living acquired during the period of high war wages, to lowered wages, and still more, to irregularities of employment. The steel strike exhausted the savings of thousands of Russians, and the fact that the coal miners were working but a few hours a day during most of the spring of 1920, also had its effect on the conditions as the writer saw them. The banks interviewed claimed that single Russians who had accounts, saved about $20 a month, but they admitted that those who patronized the banks were only a small percentage of the total Russian community. Data which seem to cast some doubt on the reliability of the consensus of opinion already given, are found in the results of the careful investigation made by the Ford Motor Company in 1917. Among 1138 Russian workmen, 917 had no bank account although this company has the reputation of paying high wages.[37] It is probable that some were not banking their money and in any case 229 were paying for the purchase of homes. The average amount on deposit, of the 221 who had bank accounts, was $563. It must

[37] From a personal statement to the author by the head of the Welfare Department of the Ford Company.

not be forgotten, however, that even not counting those who were buying a home, over half had no money in the bank even in a period of war wages. Since the statistics record 715 as married, it may be that those constituting this half were supporting families either here or abroad.

Banks

Formerly, many of the Russians kept their money with private individuals, mostly Jews, but today they more frequently deposit it in some sort of private banking institution. In every large city there are a large number of small "Russian" banks operated usually by Jews. New ones open and others close every year so that the number in any city at a given time is difficult to ascertain. In Detroit, for instance, 22 banks for Russians were opened during the war.[38] The activities of these banks cover a wide range. They may, 1—accept savings, 2—buy, sell and exchange Russian rubles, 3—send money to Russia, 4—buy and sell Liberty Bonds and Russian Loans, 5—sell steamship tickets, 6—act as notaries public for affidavits required for military service, passports, or steamship tickets, 7-give information and help on any of the following:

    (a) recommend doctors and lawyers,
    (b) lend money or write insurance,
    (c) give addresses of relatives in America,

[38] Mr. Gayman's investigation. *Cf. supra,* p. 45.

(d) give addresses of Russian-American firms,

(e) find the location of refugees, runaways, or prisoners,

(f) typewrite letters,

(g) send money to friends in America.

These banks resort to all manner of practices to get patronage. They advertise in all the Russian papers, they locate in a Russian section of the city, they use the flashiest American methods of street advertising, they keep open holidays until nine in the evening, and will often employ agents in nearby places where there is no bank. But besides these methods they try in other ways to make themselves indispensable to the Russian. Many of them, as for example, Salynak in Cleveland keep the addresses of all the Russians in the city. Others permit their bank room to be used for public lectures and meetings in Russian, which will draw the colony to their places of business. Sometimes they will go to the extent of arranging a lecture.[39] Occasionally they provide free billiards to attract customers. Mr. Gayman says that he knows of a bank in Cleveland which has even permitted prostitutes to occupy the basement in order that the bank may draw a still wider clientèle of victims.

It is obvious that banks which are operating in these ways are not in the business for anything except profit. Many of them go through voluntary bankruptcy in order to secure large secret profits. In

[39] The Spiri Bank tried to get Professor Gayman to lecture on South America in their bank.

1917 alone, in Chicago there were fourteen of these failures.[40] The Russian immigrant has rarely had experience with banking facilities and thinks that if his money is returned to him, that is all he should desire. The banks take advantage of this fact and rarely pay interest, besides taking an excessive profit on buying, selling, or exchanging Russian and American money. In every one the writer visited, the quotations were always several points dearer to the customer than in the reputable American institutions. The investigation conducted by the New York *World* and printed in that newspaper during December 1920, also corroborated that fact. One bank in San Francisco even went the length of giving out counterfeit rubles to those returning to Russia.

Sometimes the banks accept money to send to Russia when they know it cannot be delivered, as for example, in territory occupied by the Germans or the Bolsheviks. Methods illustrated by the following show the criminal practices sometimes resorted to. Through its own lawyers, a bank may spread the rumor little by little that it is insolvent. A run on the bank occurs and the establishment closes its doors. The lawyers having now won the confidence of the Russian workmen depositors, obligingly offer to get back fifty per cent of their money. Most of the Russians fall into the trap and the lawyers then divide the remainder with the bank. Accord-

[40] Mr. Gayman's investigation. *Cf. supra,* p. 45.

ing to the study conducted by Mr. Gayman, there
were in 1919 suits against such banks to the amount
of two million dollars in Baltimore alone. Although
this figure must certainly include action on behalf
of many who were not Russian Slavs, it does give
some idea of the extent of the exploitation. The
worst feature of the matter is that many of the
Russians when they have been thus exploited feel
that it is the fault of America, and they treasure
up this added grievance, while in reality it may be a
foreigner who has done the deed. "The people of
foreign countries," said the Hon. C. J. Keenan,
Deputy Appraiser of the Port of New York,
"generally look upon a bank as a government
institution, which accounts for the practice so prevalent among them of patronizing private banking
institutions after they come to this country. An
enterprising foreign-born citizen will oftentimes,
after reaching a certain stage of prosperity, open a
bank with the legend 'State Bank' over the door." [41]
Naturally whatever happens in this bank is at-
tributed to the government.

The reason why the Russians do not, to any
extent, patronize our sound financial institutions
such as national or postal savings banks is that most
of these do not have Russian interpreters and do not
try to reach the Russian through foreign language
advertising. In cities where a large bank has at-

---

[41] Davis, *Immigration and Americanization* (Boston, 1920),
p. 730.

tempted to secure Russian business in these ways it has usually succeeded and some have in the aggregate very large deposits from such sources.

But it seems probable that more Russians have been exploited by dishonest agencies than have been helped by reliable banks. On the whole, the experience of the Russian with financial institutions here has not been so favorable as to increase his respect and admiration for America.

Conditions on the Farms

Here and there throughout America are to be found Russians who have either broken away from the industrial world or else have gone directly into agriculture. The conditions confronting them have often been severe at the start, but, with a fair chance, their love of the soil and untiring industry have carried them through. For example, the colony of Stundists in North Dakota now numbers over 10,000. They even have their own little towns, one of which is named after Kiev, in Russia. Their venture has become a marked success and the colony is deeply loyal to America.

There are other settlements in South Dakota, California, Arizona, New Mexico, and Texas. Florida, Ohio, Indiana and Michigan also have a few. In Virginia there is a colony of about fifty families, nearly every one of which has one thousand dollars in the bank and some have property worth fifty to seventy thousand dollars.[42] Most of the families own their own houses which are built after the American style.

The attempts at farming have not all been successful, it is true. Where the soil has been very poor or in cases of deception and fraud, the Russian has gone back to industry. To cite but one instance, a Russian workman in California writing to a government bureau about his experience said, "I do not dream of buying a farm any more. I have tried it twice." The first time he was swindled out of his money with a forged document. The second time, a seemingly official "Russian American agent" in Salt Lake City who showed fine specimens of fruit and vegetables, and "photographs of good cattle and splendid fields," offered this land at $25 an acre. So he with other Russians sold their houses and bought the property.

When we arrived we found a waterless desert. Several returned immediately seeing their mistake but about thirty families remained, tilling the soil and suffering hunger. Soon they saw what they had planted did not grow, and were obliged to leave everything and go to the nearest cities in order to earn money. That is what happens to the Russian people in America.[43]

Some of the Russians are more shrewd and send

[42] Mr. Gayman's investigation. *Cf. supra.,* p. 45.
[43] From a letter written to the Governmental Information Bureau of the Committee on Public Information, of which the writer has a copy.

one of their number to see the property before purchasing it, but even then they occasionally are cheated through legal technicalities.

Those Russians who do locate on good soil usually believe in America. The contrast with the tyrannical conditions in Russia is so great that they are happy. M. I. Wolkoff, a Russian professor in the College of Agriculture of the University of Illinois, testifies that the Russians on the land are "the most contented" of any in America. "They are much better off financially than their city countrymen, and perhaps this is one of the chief reasons." [44] Undoubtedly another is that they are free to work as they please and are engaged in an occupation which they like. On the land, moreover, although somewhat isolated from Americans since they tend to settle in groups, they at least see a favorable side of our country. It is therefore to be regretted that those engaged in agriculture are but a small fraction of the number here. Russian authorities estimate that over 90 per cent of the Russians in the United States are working in our industries and mines. [45] The very fact that the Russians can be made to like America so easily if they have a fair chance, together with the fact that we sorely need agricultural workers, makes it seem all the more deplorable that little is done to assist them

[44] Letter to the author.
[45] The Secretary to the Russian Consul General, E. I. Hourwich, M. Vilchur, and others.

to become farmers or to make them more contented in industry.

Conclusion

In this chapter we have been describing the reactions of the typical Russian worker. It is true, there are some industries and some instances even in steel and coal mining where the Russian is happy and successful in his work. But as we have seen, the majority are plunged into an environment totally at variance with their European background. The economic forces in the situation provide little outlet for their legitimate instinctive responses. Especially does their situation give little opportunity for what Giddings calls the "desire for recognition" or for what McDougall speaks of as self-assertion and Thorndike as mastery. The lowest of the labor group, they feel that regardless of how well or faithfully they work there is no opportunity for them to rise; that they will always be looked down on by Americans. This fact, and the total absence of information about the men higher up, together with a growing conviction that their human side is totally disregarded, is what Russian workers have so often tried to express to the writer. The solitary favorable factor, the amount of the wage, is too often destroyed by exploiting or dishonest banks or agencies which swindle the hard working and thrifty ones out of their earnings. It is true, moreover, that as fast as they adopt American standards, their margin of savings dwindles or disappears.

American industry has rendered a tremendous service in giving employment to aliens from other lands where poverty, disease and tyranny prevail, and in turning out more goods than any other nation and thus enriching the entire world. Yet we must remember that the great structure of American industry has been built upon the brawn, indeed, the very lives of foreigners. Business men and writers agree that Americans would hardly be willing at any price to do the work these foreign-born are doing. Since we sorely need what they have to give, is it any more than just that the economic forces which condition their success as workers and their well-being as men should be a help rather than a hindrance?

CHAPTER IV

WE have glanced briefly at the influences which mold the Russian's life in the economic world. As we turn now to his social environment, one of the outstanding facts is that he is effectively cut off from most of our own contacts with American life.

Isolation

In nearly every city the Russians live in a group by themselves. When they first come to a community they naturally gravitate to the poorest sections where rents are cheapest. A process of segregation results, for race prejudice, strange customs, and language barriers all make the American loath to live close to these Slavic immigrants. Heterogeneous America has, to some extent, a social stratification based on likenesses in income and nationality. Once a district has begun to be invaded by the Russians, Americans avoid it and other Russians follow where their own kind already are. Usually the Russian-speaking Jews settle in a locality first and are followed by the Russian Slavs. Thus Pittsburgh has her Soho District and the neighborhood around Pennsylvania Avenue and Mulberry Street. Even in the mining towns, the Russian shacks tend to crowd together into a definite group. Like follows like. This sociological law is as true to-day as it was when the ancient maxim about "birds of a feather" first found expression. The Russian district is peopled almost entirely by the foreign-born, and whether it be housing accommodations, food supplies, or medical aid that the immigrant seeks, he is likely to meet the foreigner almost exclusively. Yet his impressions and opinion of America become deeply affected by his experience in these "alien" centers.

Housing

Housing conditions vary according to the colony. In the agricultural districts, where the Russians are not migratory workers, they usually own their own dwellings. Many of these houses may be favorably compared with those of Americans. In the mining communities the Russians rent and occasionally buy small houses. In the study of Russian households which was made by the U. S. Immigration Commission in 1909,[1] out of 83 studied only one house was owned by the occupant. Since then, however, the percentage may have increased considerably. For instance, among 50 Russian families investigated in Los Angeles in 1915, 26 owned their own homes.[2] The average value was about two thousand dollars. In 1917 in Detroit, among the 1160 Russian em-

[1] Abstract, vol. 1, table 89, *op. cit.*, p. 467.
[2] Sokoloff, L., *The Russians in Los Angeles* (Los Angeles, 1918), p. 6.

ployees of the Ford plant, eighteen owned their own homes and 229 were buying theirs—a fact which is considered exceptional. As is usually the case where the tenants are the owners, the houses are in better repair, are cleaner and more sanitary than rented ones, possibly because those who buy are the more progressive foreigners. The great majority of Russians, however, still live in rented rooms in tenement houses.

Because overcrowding is common in the homeland, Russians are willing to accept similar or worse conditions here. In the United States Immigration Commission's study,[3] out of 75 Russian households there was an average of 2.85 persons per sleeping room, the general average for the total foreign-born being 2.53. Mr. Cole in his Chicago study of 1919[4] found that only 35 per cent of the single Russians and 18 per cent of the family Russians had in their sleeping rooms the 400 cubic feet of air per person required by the city ordinance. In the same report he states that out of 30 apartments occupied by Russians there was an average of 7.2 individuals living in an average apartment of 4.3 rooms. Eleven of these were front apartments, while 14 were in the rear; four occupied a whole floor and one was in the center. Sixty of 85 rooms had only one window each, 23 had two, one had four, and one alcove room had none. Approximately half were so dark or

[3] Abstract, vol. 1, table 72, *op. cit.,* p. 430.
[4] *Cf. supra,* chap. iii, p. 34.

gloomy that on a bright day one could not read in
the center of the room. Eighteen families had
toilets in their own apartments. Eleven had hall
toilets, shared by eight to nineteen neighbors, and
one had the toilet in the yard, which was also used
by twelve outsiders. Only two of the thirty had a
bath tub; in one of these cases the tub was used for
laundry purposes. The author's investigation in the
various Russian communities showed that the overwhelming number of Russians are living in the worst
type of tenement apartments. These have but few
windows and no baths. The homes occupied by Russian workers employed at the Ford plant in Detroit
in 1917 were an exception. Out of 1160, 978 had
good homes, 157 fair and 25 poor.[5] As the chief
standard here considered, however, was cleanliness,
and as the Ford plant attracts the best type of
worker, this does not necessarily imply that there
was no overcrowding or that these cases are typical.

The homes seen in Pittsburgh are perhaps a fairer
sample. In one apartment of three rooms, a Russian family of five was paying $17 a month. This
was to be increased to $20 on May 1, 1920. There
was one inside room where all the family slept,
which was entirely without windows and was heated
by an ill-smelling gas stove. The second room was
used by five boarders, each of whom paid six dollars
a month for the privilege. The other was a kitchen,
laundry, and living room all in one. In one apart-

[5] From an investigation made by the Ford Company in 1917.

ment of four rooms in a frame tenement near the
steel mills the family, consisting of father, mother,
and four children, slept in one room and seven men
slept in the other three. All the windows were
closed, and the floor served as a common spitoon.
The rent for the bare dilapidated rooms without
heat was $18 a month. Large cracks in the wall were
stuffed with rags, a motley array of clothes was
hanging in the room to dry. This was representative
of many apartments in Pittsburgh.[6]

Michael M. Davis in his study of *Immigrant
Health and the Community* for the Carnegie Americanization studies describes the various types of
tenements inhabited by foreigners and concludes,
"Wretched and unsanitary housing is not the immigrants' responsibility alone. The native American
must bear a large share of the blame." He gives
a fair picture of the Russian huts in some of the
mining districts: "The coal and iron mining regions
of the country to which so many of the Finns and
Slavic peoples turn, show some of our worst housing
conditions. Shacks are built both by individuals
and by mining companies close to mine shafts, pits
and coke ovens. Tin cans, tar paper, and old boards
furnish building materials for crazy shelters. Into
one or more small rooms crowd the large families
of the workmen. Toilets are either absent, or else

---

[6] According to the statement of the Russian worker at the International Institute. The writer, himself, saw at least ten of this
description, out of forty or more visited.

miserable privies are erected and neglected. Outdoor pumps furnish water, and the ground surface serves as a sewer." [7]

In some construction and laboring work the companies still provide barracks for the men. Although they vary considerably, perhaps the following quotation describing foreign bunk-houses which sometimes contained 36 men in 3-tier bunks, from Francis A. Kellor, the secretary of the Inter-Racial Council, is typical. "These are rather dark, having been finished in creosote to keep down the vermin. Some are heated with stoves, all built upon posts, not very clean—and represent an outlay of $20 per employee housed, exclusive of ground and ground improvements. There is a sink outside with sewer connections for slops, and shower baths and toilets at the end of each row." [8] Several college graduates who worked in the lumber camps of Washington in 1920 gave similar descriptions but added that the barracks were never cleaned, so that a shovel would have been more effective than a broom. Where they worked, moreover, there were no shower baths. The Russian priest in Cleveland even tells of one of his families which lives in a freight car, and of his christening a baby born there. The writer has interviewed several groups of single Russians who were living in similar lodgings, but these are exceptional. In every such case they were working for

[7] From a manuscript copy transmitted to the author.
[8] *The Immigrants in America Review,* April, 1916.

the railroad and when they left the company's employ had to leave their domicile.

The accommodations of Russians in New York are perhaps more varied than in most other cities. But if one cares to visit the throbbing, dusty district of lower Second Avenue and has the courage to enter one of the small side doors and to climb a dark, narrow stairway of two flights, he can see one type. The plaster is cracked and here and there are spots where it has broken off, thus adding to the dust on the floor. The apartment consists of one room about ten by fourteen feet and an alcove seven by six feet shut off by heavy curtains and containing a double bed. The room has two windows opening on a fire escape, but the alcove bedroom has none. For this room—including only the bare walls and the sink—eleven dollars a month are paid. The small coal stove, the few chairs, a cheap chiffonier and the bed, all belong to the family. Of course there is no toilet except the one in the hall which is shared by the other families. The apartments on Cherry Street are in a poorer locality, the refuse on the streets is scattered about, and the saloons still sell cheap liquor.[9] While some of the apartments are worse than those already described, the majority are larger, but have more dark rooms and a generous assortment of lodgers who fill up the extra space.

In Boston the living conditions of the Russians

[9] February, 1921.

resemble those we have described; the rooms and corridors are dark, with little ventilation and much overcrowding. There is the usual common toilet and in some cases the apartments do not even have running water. One Russian, speaking before the Volstead Act became operative, expressed his reaction to the conditions by saying, "We don't see anything but saloons, and factories, and bad housing in America."

There are, of course, communities where the housing conditions are much better, such as those we have mentioned in California and Detroit. But it is obvious that the vast majority of places present a decided contrast to the villages of Russia. There, in spite of dirt, at least the open fields were near and sunshine and fresh air abundant. The priest in Hartford reports that some of the more energetic Russians in his locality are so desirous of getting reasonable lodgings in the country that they will rent places in New Hampshire, thus necessitating three changes of electric cars in reaching their work. Besides this they must get up at four in the morning and do not return till nearly ten at night; but each one has a little garden which adds to the attraction of the Sunday holiday. The majority accept the bad housing as one of the handicaps to life in America.

One can hardly wonder that Dr. John Kulzzyszki, a practicing Ukranian physician in Scranton told the author:

The greatest thing that America can do for the foreigners
is to control the renting of houses.   Americans build holes
which are not fit for the pigs to live in, and rent them out
to Russians.   People say the Russians live badly because
they live that way in Russia, but there they were compelled
to live so; here they should have a chance to improve.

Undoubtedly, part of the blame for these conditions is due to the lack of initiative of the Russians,
but certainly it is no credit to our social order that
more is not done to help educate them to better
standards, or to compel the American owners to
make decency possible for their tenants.   That the
housing conditions provided for the Russians were
just as poor as the owners dared to have them, was
the opinion of the United States Immigration Commissioner in Pittsburgh.

Frequently the person who collects the rent may
be a foreigner, but as the Russians say, "How can
we tell?   He speaks English, he is an American to
us."   The agent, according to the Russians, rarely
agrees to make any improvements, although they
may be sorely needed.   Few tenants dare to insist,
for they may receive a request for an increase of
rent by way of reply.   One priest told me his experience with these agents:

When they are Americans they are very polite as long
as they think they can get your money.   One insurance
agent crossed himself as he opened my door.   After he received my order he went out slamming the door and spitting

on the porch. When others come for the rent, they will offer me a cigarette; when they have no business, they won't even recognize me on the street.

The average worker does not care especially for recognition by an agent, but often he isn't treated even decently, and if he is at all delinquent in his payments he is likely to find himself on the street.

Not only does this isolation and bad housing separate the Russian from Americans, but he feels that he is regarded as an inferior. The expansion of his consciousness of kind to include Americans is hindered or wholly prevented. Americans do not show any sympathy for him nor does his tenement life give opportunity to gratify his desire for a reasonable amount of recognition. The Russian sees little opportunity for the expression of his ego or of his pride in family or home. Woodworth believes that most human mechanisms, once aroused, are capable of furnishing their own drive and of lending drive to other connected mechanisms.[10] But as we have already seen, the mechanism of the Russian has little chance in his daily task either to respond to the drive of certain instincts or to give expression to his native capacities. These instincts and capacities suppressed in the industrial field might conceivably find an outlet in his home life. But here he is living in a sordid environment of

[10] Woodworth, R. S., *Dynamic Psychology* (N. Y., 1918), pp. 36-43.

cheap tenements—ugly or dilapidated—with their accompaniment of congestion, noise, and dirt. Americans look askance at the "Dagoes" and "Polacks." The Russian feels this if he goes into an American shop to trade; he notes it in the attitude of the rent collector. It is impossible to say how far this condition creates in the Russian a dislike for our country, but it is one decided factor which cannot be overlooked.

No matter what the angle of approach to the housing conditions and the associations incidental to them, the conclusion is inevitable that a large majority of the Russians have here little or no opportunity for favorable contacts with Americans.

Factors Relating to Health

The Russian's food is usually purchased in a Jewish grocery or meat market in his neighborhood. The turnover is not large and the proprietor makes as much as the traffic will bear. As tested by the writer, prices were always higher for the same quality of goods than in the better grade of grocery stores for Americans. It was, of course, extremely difficult to make sure of the same quality, but it was interesting to find that a cheap grade of butter cost less at the large American store than at the foreign one.

In the Jewish grocery the same brand of flour was higher per pound, while certain brands of cereals and canned goods were three or four cents more.   Mr. Sibray, the U. S. Immigration Commissioner in Pittsburgh, says that we charge the foreigner decidedly more than we charge ourselves.   A Russian-Jewish storekeeper in Detroit explained that these high prices were due to capitalistic profiteering, and Russian workmen seldom account for the high prices in any other way.   To offset them, the small shopkeepers often buy food of the lowest grade; stale meat and withered vegetables.   The Russian has been used to fresh food, the products of his own fields, but here in the market, accessible to him, the same articles are few, old and expensive. He is likely therefore to change his diet to one consisting largely of meat of questionable age, the quality of which is less noticeable to him.   The wife of the priest in Hartford tells of seeing one Russian boarding-house keeper in 1920 buy 27 pounds of meat for $1.50.   It was the cheapest there was, for the butcher picked it out from the scraps under the table.   A heavy meat diet is undoubtedly responsible for a great deal of digestive trouble among the Russians, and Jewish doctors with whom the writer consulted stated that this malady was the most common cause of complaint.   There are few other single factors which are more potent in contributing to discontent than poor food and a disordered stomach.   In giving his opinion of the greatest need of the Russians to a government bureau, one Russian from Gary, Indiana, wrote, "We need fresh food products and fresh meat and there is no such meat

now in America." [11]   He judged, of course, only
from his own limited experience.

Nearly all the doctors who were consulted mentioned tuberculosis also and venereal disease as existing, but perhaps not to a greater extent than
among other races. They thought that the factory
work with its absence of outdoor healthful labor
and its contrast to field work cannot but increase
the prevalence of tuberculosis, as the absence of
normal family life has increased venereal disease.
The fact that, as a rule, only the strongest Russians
migrate to America minimizes the prevalence of disease to an extent difficult to estimate. It seemed to
be the opinion of the Russians in the mining and
steel industries that more were laid off on account
of accidents than by illness. Statistics by nationality
are extremely difficult to secure from the hospitals,
and when obtained are not very reliable for the Russian, since so many patronize private doctors.

A study conducted by Dr. E. H. Lewinsky-Cor-
win under the auspices of the New York Academy
of Medicine in 1919 among 8,645 individuals and
2,023 families of which 357 families and 1,692 individuals were Slavs, showed that over ten per cent
of the Slavs were ill at the time of the investigation.
This was double the percentage for the Italians and
was, next to the Irish, the highest. It is significant
that the Slavs used the dispensary in only 2.2 per
cent of their cases, the general hospital in only 2.3

[11] From a letter of which the author has a copy.

per cent and did not use the maternity hospital at all. They avail themselves of institutional help less than any of the other nationalities; in fact, not quite one half as frequently as the next in order, the Italians. On the other hand, 58.2 per cent secure the services of private physicians. This is the largest percentage with the exception of the Italians, while in 35 per cent of all the cases they utilize a midwife, a druggist, or depend on themselves—a higher proportion than in any other group. Considering only confinement cases, 87.5 per cent of the Slavs employed a midwife, the same percentage as for the Italians and more than for any other race. In minor complaints such as colds, stomach trouble or being "run down," 58 per cent of the Slavs visited private physicians, more than any other nationality, and only 1.7 per cent used a dispensary, the lowest percentage of all. Of the remainder, 39.1 per cent depended upon non-professional care, and 1.1 per cent on their lodge or society physician.[12]

In giving their reasons for not going to a dispensary, over one-quarter of the Slavs said they did not know that such an institution existed, while the others said that they were able to pay a private doctor, or that they could not speak English, or were afraid, or were dissatisfied with the kind of treatment given, or that there was no dispensary near. It must be remembered that it is extremely

[12] Public Health Committee of the New York Academy of Medicine, *The Problem of Disease* (N. Y., 1921), pp. 1-23.

difficult to get the real reasons in such an investigation and those who replied that they were able to pay, undoubtedly had other unexpressed objections to using a dispensary. Although these statistics included other Slavic races besides the Russian, they corroborate the investigation of the author. Most Russian Slavs either do not know where to go or have never even heard that there is a dispensary. Those who might go cannot speak English, and dispensaries and hospitals rarely provide interpreters. Some seem to be prejudiced, fearing that they will be experimented on by doctors "who do not care whether we get well or die." "If you go to the hospital they poison you and cut you up for practice," is a saying occasionally heard. One man even told the writer that in the case of a friend who had gone to the free ward the doctor had used a hypodermic injection. The Russian had protested, but the doctor replied that he wanted to see how it would work on him anyway. The conclusion of the Russian, although apparently erroneous, was that the doctor was less interested in curing him than in experimenting upon him.

The effect on those who have been in our hospitals is not always so bad. For example, a Russian woman on Cherry Street in New York City, who has lived in America eighteen years and can yet speak no English because she "has not met Americans" went to Gouverneur Hospital. Her husband had been killed four years before; she was supporting her three children by cleaning one downtown office daily from three to nine A.M. for $15 a week and a dentist's office three hours in the evening for $8 a week. On this money she lived in a dark little apartment of three rooms. The ceiling was mildewed and the plaster was falling off. Only the room which she rented out had direct access to the fresh air. She became afflicted with severe pains and the Jewish doctor informed her that the trouble was appendicitis. An operation was too expensive, so she continued her work, but her condition finally became so serious that she was confined to her bed. A boarder called a policeman, who, in turn, summoned an ambulance, and an operation in the hospital followed. After she was discharged, the institution continued to look out for her welfare by sending her a box of supplies and a daily bottle of milk. This one friendly experience has made her an enthusiastic believer in America.

In the absence of hospital data about diseases among the Russians, the testimony of priests and Russian-speaking doctors in the following places is worth recording as, perhaps, representative.

From Connecticut: "In the cotton mills there is little ventilation, the air is saturated with small particles of cotton fiber. Few Russians can work more than four years in this environment. In the rubber factories, the fumes from the acids bring on disease and in the majority of cases after six years they lose their health."

"In the rubber company after three years they get sick from tuberculosis from the acid fumes."

From Pennsylvania: "In steel if he is working twelve hours a day, the ordinary Russian is absolutely used up in a few years. One example is Sapitsky, who worked six years at the Crucible Steel carrying heavy steel bars. He has now been in the hospital a year."

"In the mines tuberculosis is common. I have just come from the home of a Russian who has been here fifteen years. He is forty-nine years old, and has eight children, and is dying of tuberculosis."

"The custom in America of sleeping on mattresses simply results in providing a better breeding ground for vermin. The housing conditions are so bad the Russians get sick."

"In Russia they have clean food and good vegetables so they can eat them without washing. Here in America the Russian buys the worst and it is full of disease."

"Not healthy work, all die young. There is not one who has lived to be sixty in my parish."

From Akron: "While improving on the financial side the Russian is deteriorating on the physical side."

"Rubber works are hard on the teeth. Tuberculosis and venereal disease exist in spite of the naturally strong constitution of the Russian."

From Lawrence: "The Russian is constitutionally strong, but the textile industry is very dusty and is hard on the lungs; the longer he remains, the more prone he is to tuberculosis."

From Cleveland: "The most prevalent disease among the Russians is tuberculosis."

Whether or not these are accurate observations, they do indicate what Russians believe to be true, namely, that, in their situation, America is not a healthy place to live in. Most of the Russians admit that our cities are cleaner than those of Russia and that the water supply and sewage system are something they did not have at home. But these advantages do not seem to impress themselves with great force on the Russian from the village; he points to the loss in his own weight as an index of the deleterious effect of America. One will frequently say, "I was one hundred and seventy pounds in weight, now I am only one hundred and thirty," or "I weighed two hundred pounds, now I am only one hundred and forty."

What makes ill health worse for the Russian is that he has no family physician to whom he can turn. Rarely speaking English, he must patronize those who can understand him, and these are often quack doctors who use every device for ensnaring him. The editor of one of the Russian newspapers told me that his paper only kept running from the advertisements of these "leeches." Another stated that his paper secured thirty per cent of its income from medical advertisements. Yet after an analysis of medical advertisements in Russian papers, Mi-

chael M. Davis of the Boston Dispensary and head
of the department of Health Standards of the
Americanization Studies of the Carnegie Foundation, says that they are "very obviously fakes."
Here is a sample of one advertisement translated
into English. "This is the only doctor from the
old country—— Fellow citizens: look for help
where you can find it, which will bring you out on
the right path. This is the only doctor from the
old country. He speaks Russian and has a practice
of twenty-five years. He cures with the best remedies, chronic and all diseases. Do not lose any time.
Come promptly to his office. Advice free." Another
reads: "Do you suffer from weak nerves, lame back,
forgetfulness, palpitation of the heart, weak lungs,
dull heavy feeling, headache, dizziness, dimness of
vision, weakness of limbs, ulcers, sores, catarrh,
dripping in the throat, pain in the stomach or back,
sore throat, coated tongue, constipation, rheumatic
pains, pimples? These and many others are the first
warnings of the loss of health. Come to me at once,
if you need treatment. Delays are dangerous. No
disease lies dormant."

The Russians testify that they never go to these
doctors without learning that they have a serious
complaint, and paying a good round sum. A Polish
doctor told me that quack doctors frequently scare
the Russians into the belief that they have serious
maladies and then charge them as much as they will

bear. A Jewish doctor told me that the Russians always pay whatever he asks without a murmur and that he greatly preferred them to Americans, who always make trouble over the bill. Although the Russians report going to German, Polish, Jewish, colored and even Japanese doctors they seldom consult an American one. In answer to my question as to where he secured a brilliant scarlet-colored fluid for spraying his nose, a Russian worker in Philadelphia replied that it came from a negro doctor. "He charges less than the Jewish one," was his reason for patronizing him. Another described his preference for a Jewish dentist. "The American one says, 'Hurry up, get a jump, open your mouth wide, hold up your head high.' In fifteen minutes the work was done. The Jewish doctor takes an hour and does the job good." Still another told me that an American dentist pulled out the wrong tooth. When he went back the dentist said, "Well, I was busy and didn't notice." After finally pulling out the right one, this man charged him for both teeth. Whether true or not, this story reflects the narrator's state of mind.

In addition to his experience with the doctors, the Russian, along with everybody else, is exposed to the patent medicine danger, only he has not been educated with regard to its injurious effects. Here is a specimen advertisement:

EVERY RUSSIAN MOTHER

knows that the only certain medicine for the crying and discomfort and sleeplessness of her baby is "Romko," manufactured by the Baby Safety Company. Do not let your baby cry and suffer for hours. If your child has a stomach ache or suffers from constipation; if its teeth are coming and it is sick for this reason; if it cries and is discontented, do not wait one minute, but buy in the local drug store, for thirty-five cents, a bottle of "Romko," manufactured by the Baby Safety Company. If you cannot get the original there, send a paper dollar for three bottles, or stamps for thirty-five cents for one bottle, to the following address: . . . . [13]

To all too many Russians, patent medicines and quack doctors are another side of America which stands for money-getting rather than friendship. Perhaps the chief charges the Russians lay up against America on the side of their health are:

1. The climate is bad. The damp atmosphere with the alternating hot and cold temperatures is far different from the dry cold of Russia.

2. The change from the open fields to the factory air surcharged with chemical fumes, dust and other impurities is a radical one.

3. The unsanitary tenement houses with the resultant overcrowding, breed disease.

4. The constant meat diet, as contrasted with the

---

[13] Advertisement given to the author in translated form by Michael M. Davis, of the Carnegie Americanization Studies.

fresh vegetables of the Russian peasant, is harmful.

5. The exploitation of quack doctors makes them a prey to greed when they most need help.

It is a matter of common knowledge that individuals who do not have the right diet, or are below par physically are inclined to be pessimistic toward all their environmental situation. Now the Russian, as we have just noted, has come from a different climate with different food and from an outdoor life into factory conditions and tenement congestion. These things cannot but affect his health. If, in addition to this, he is exploited by the foreign doctor to whom he turns for help, his mental reaction may be prejudiced against every situation in which he is placed. This factor alone might predispose him to dislike America. It certainly leaves him open minded towards radical propaganda, which always bitterly assails the existing conditions.

Single Russians

The overwhelming majority of Russians in this country are single, or without wives here. In the Immigration Commission Report of 1909, 41.4 per cent of the 6,621 Russians twenty years of age or over were single. Out of the entire number there were only 140 married Russian women, a fact tending to indicate that the wives of the great majority of married males were still in Europe. From 1898 until the outbreak of the war, 14 per cent of the Russian immigration has been female and 86 per

cent male. This means that on entering the United
States at least seventy-two per cent of the Russians
were single or without their wives.[14]

This paucity of Russian women results, to some
extent, in a suppression of normal sex responses.
These tendencies must either be repressed entirely
or find expression in abnormal ways which American *mores* prohibit. The frequent advertisements
in the Russian press asking for news of the where-
abouts of a wife who has run away with one of the
boarders is but one index of this situation. "Freud
considers that the origin of all cases belonging to
certain varieties of mental disease can be traced back
to factors connected with a single one of the great
instincts, that of sex." [15] While Freud is considered
by many to have overemphasized the rôle of sex,
few would deny that in many cases his explanation
has a large measure of truth. The suppression of
the normal opportunity for sex responses in the Russian is one more factor which affects his attitude.

In addition to this fact, the single Russian has
few contacts with the favorable side of American
life. He usually secures his room from foreigners
and makes his living arrangements in one of the following ways:

a—By renting a room and boarding himself.

[14] U. S. Bureau of Immigration, *Annual Report of the Commissioner General of Immigration* for each year from 1898-1914,
table 7.

[15] Hart, B., *The Psychology of Insanity* (Cambridge, England,
1912), p. 166.

b—By renting a room and boarding at the restaurants.

c—By renting rooms coöperatively with other Russians. In this case members of the group eat chiefly at restaurants, but take supper and Sunday meals together in their rooms. Often they have no system in their buying. First one man makes a purchase, then another, and each time the cost is divided.

d—By boarding in a family where the landlady does the cooking and the washing. There are several ways of paying for the board. Sometimes, although rarely, there is a flat rate, in which case the landlady keeps no books. In other cases she buys all the food and once every two weeks the total bill is divided. Another method is for each man to have his own account book; the landlady purchases what he wants and charges it to him.

In Mr. Cole's Chicago study,[16] the average wage of the single men was only $23 a week and fifty-one per cent were spending $20 or over each week. In contrast to the married Russians they often buy expensive clothes and enjoy a heavy diet in restaurants. This was the daily food ration of some of these workmen in Pittsburgh: at 5 A. M., coffee and bread; at 9 A. M., "on the sly," so they say, sausage (*culbasa*), bread and perhaps an apple; at noon, coffee, steak, and bread; and at six o'clock cabbage soup, one-half pound of meat, bread and potatoes. Others interviewed had coffee with eggs or ham in the morning; sausage, bread and butter and apple pie at noon; and half a pound of meat

---

[16] *Cf. supra,* chap. iii, p. 34.

with soup and bread at night. In New York City the patronage of cheap foreign restaurants seems to be almost universal. The ones utilized are mostly Jewish. For example, in Brownsville, a Jewish-Russian section of Brooklyn, there are only two Russian and two Polish restaurants, although there are a great many places where the Russians eat, the proprietors of which are foreign-born Jews. The result is that patronizing a restaurant does not ordinarily bring Russians into contact with Americans. Russians with whom the writer talked in New York City in 1921 claimed that their food cost them from $1.40 to $2.00 daily per person. Apparently, they can live more cheaply than Americans chiefly because they are willing to put up with congested quarters and low rents. These very conditions, however, keep them isolated from American life in an alien environment which by them is falsely thought of as typifying America.

Married Russians

We have already shown that the overwhelming majority of Russians in America are single or without their wives. The scarcity value of the Russian women who are here is well illustrated by the following incident. A young woman inserted an advertisement in the Russian paper for a secretarial position; within a week she had received over fifty replies asking for her hand in marriage. The result of the scarcity of Russian girls is that there is some intermarriage with Ruthenians, Poles or any Slavic nationality.

It is obvious that life in congested and dilapidated tenements cannot be ideal. For many married Russians the sitting room, kitchen and bedroom are all in one. The writer visited a family of five who were living in this way. The husband worked twelve hours a night and was sound asleep at eleven in the morning, oblivious to his caller or the children. The wife contributed her share toward the support of the family by renting her other room to boarders. The apartment of two rooms cost sixteen dollars a month. The walls were mildewed and in spots the paper hung down in tatters, and it is obvious that little wholesome family life can exist in such a house —yet there are many such Russian homes. The two older children attend an American public school; their last report cards showed a good record. They get no help from their parents, who are illiterate. Both these children enjoyed school; but as soon as possible they will be sent to work in order to contribute their share towards the family income. I went over the expenses of the family with the mother and found that they were not saving a cent. The cost of food and clothes for the children, who wanted to be dressed as well as the others in the school, made saving impossible.

The women work exceptionally hard. For example, one known to the writer cares for seven children and eighteen boarders. She gets up at six A. M.

and works until night, cooking, washing, and scrubbing daily for twenty-seven people, yet she thinks she is not doing over much. Nearly all the women either take in boarders or do outside work, and some do both. In Ansonia, Connecticut, for example, some of the mothers sew on buttons; in Philadelphia they frequently work in the candy or cigar factories. One family there adopted the plan of having the husband at his job during the night and the wife during the day, so that some one was at home with the children all the time. In Boston and Lawrence the women are in the spinning mills and candy factories. In some of the mining towns they keep a few chickens, selling the eggs. In Hartford the priest said that many of the women string tobacco. Wherever they are, the women find extra tasks, and their lot is not easy.

Frequently the husband will start away at eight in the morning and be back at six in the evening; but the wife must have the breakfast ready before the men leave and then care for the children all day; perhaps, also, doing some sewing for a clothing concern. She must purchase the groceries, wash the clothes, clean and cook, not only for her own family but for the boarders as well. The pall of heavy, monotonous labor lies upon the entire family. The men return from the day's labor in blast furnace or mine tired out and incapable of any real comradeship with their children or wives. In the family relationships, then, the Russians are, as a rule, isolated from wholesome influences except those which may come through the children who attend the public school.

The Second Generation

The Russian children, as a whole, know English better than they do Russian. They will understand when their parents speak in the Old Country tongue, but will usually answer in English. They attend the public schools until they can pass muster as old enough to work. Considerable violation of the school law occurs, because, although the Russians take pride in their children and wish them to secure better jobs and live easier lives than they have, economic pressure is too strong for them. As far as they can, the children dress like American children and often look askance at the peculiar habits and customs of their parents. A common schooling breaks down a good deal of racial prejudice, and the children mingle with almost any of those in the neighborhood, even the blacks.

All too early, however, they must begin to contribute their share to the family income as office boys, clerks, candy-factory workers, errand or messenger boys, drivers, and what not. The girls often work at the bargain counter at an extremely low wage, which they feel is inadequate for their needs. They do not know how to spend their money wisely and naturally desire the silks and furs which are worn by others at the dances, their chief amusement.

It is seldom that they are not able to purchase some of these clothes, but often it is at the expense of their food.

The young Russians of the second generation, in so far as they have gone to our public schools, have come in touch with some of the wholesome influences of our American life, and they respond with appreciation. They feel more American than Russian. Unfortunately, the majority leave school somewhere between the sixth and eighth grades with hardly more than the barest rudiments of reading and writing, and are destined to live among the lowest ranks of our citizens.[17]

Recreation

Mr. Cole in a tabulation of the predominant recreational interests of ninety-eight Russian men in Chicago[18] notes that sixteen claimed the saloon and more than half of the entire number frequented it; next came the movies with thirteen, although nearly all stated that they attended occasionally.

The other interests follow in the order of their importance: Reading 13, dancing 11, music 11, home 6, girls 5, church 5, walking 4, bowling 4, theater 3, pool 3, cards 2, meetings 2. The men who worked seven days a week were very bitter

[17] The Russian is among the newest of our immigrants. There has not yet been time for a large number of the second generation to grow up in our country, and this study is primarily concerned with the foreign-born.

[18] *Cf. supra,* chap. iii, p. 34. (Mr. Cole secured data on their recreational interests from 98 out of the 112 men investigated.)

when asked, "What do you do when you want to have a good time?" One said, "When we want a good time, sleep a couple of hours." Another said, "We work like bull, no time even for rest."

The prohibition amendment has brought a change in the recreational life of many Russians. Although they can still purchase liquor in some places, it is expensive. Some have begun to make their own liquor at home, but this is by no means universally true. In one mining town in Pennsylvania the authorities stated that in the days of the saloon they had to keep a special policeman all the time to handle the drunken quarrels arising among the Russians and Ruthenians. Now they have no policeman at all. Our American civic and religious forces have, as yet, put nothing in the place of the saloon, and the Russian spends his time as best he can. Probably the greatest single number patronize the moving picture houses; nearly all the Russians go occasionally.

The cases of Russians arrested in the Communist raids may be somewhat exceptional, and yet they are significant. Out of 40 men interviewed, 18 had been accustomed to attend the movies once a week or oftener and the theater once or more in two weeks. Nine of these had gone on an average of 2.7 times a week. The other twenty-two varied widely, eleven patronizing a performance once in two weeks or a month, while the rest attended but rarely. Those who frequented the movies over twice a week went to the theater about three times a month. As might be expected, the foreigners usually patronize the smaller shows. The character of the pictures as seen by the writer was largely of the sex appeal mingled with the dime novel mystery and murder. One Russian workman in Akron characterized them as "only play, killing and jumping." Often they depict the life of millionaires living in idleness and luxury, and naturally the Russian who seldom comes into contact with real Americans often forms a part of his conception of American life from what he sees in the pictures. They make him think of the contrast between his own surroundings and those portrayed in the film.

Card playing is a constant source of amusement. Many of the Russians play at home and often there is the added incentive of money stakes. This is hardly to be wondered at, for when they cannot read they have few other amusements.

Dances are frequently given among the Russians and are largely patronized by the younger men and women. Occasionally, also, amateur theatricals are staged. Most of the Russians love music; the *balalaika* [19] and other stringed instruments are popular. The beautiful Russian folksongs and the music from their own celebrated masters—Tschaikowsky, for example—present a striking contrast to our American ragtime. It is no wonder that the Russian appre-

[19] The *balalaika* is a Russian musical instrument resembling a guitar.

ciates his own music and that in the dark city tenements he will occasionally recall his homeland in such verses as these:

ON THE BANKS OF THE VOLGA [20]

On the waters of our little-mother Volga
The storm is lashing, and the waves rise high;
Alone a tiny boat is battling
Alone 'midst the fury of the gale;
But look! at the helm there stands a figure,
Scorning death in the waters dark and grim,
'Tis the hero of our little-mother Volga
Our Stegneka Rasine.

THE FAIR LITTLE MEADOW

O meadow, fair little meadow, wide in sweep, wide in sweep,
On thee, fair, dear meadow, the shadows descend, the shadows descend,
The lad loved a lass, loved with a love not of earth, but profound.

So few are the Russian gathering places that comparatively seldom do the Russians join together for a Sunday walk as in Russia. Until the wholesale arrests by our Federal authorities in 1920,[21] many of the Russians attended small political clubs and meetings; after that, group meetings were, for a time, precarious and consequently secret, but now, in 1922, they are beginning again.

[20] From a translation by Miss Isabel Hapgood, used on the program of a Russian musicale in New York in 1921.
[21] This refers to general arrests directed against Communists and alien radicals. *Cf.* chap. vi.

In the agricultural districts the dearth of entertainment is even more apparent. Perhaps it has not been an entire loss that in so many rural communities the modern brand of moving pictures has been lacking.

In associative recreation as well as in other forms of group activity, the basic factor is consciousness of kind. Those that are alike tend to associate together. There is what Woodworth calls a social impulse, "an impulse to act together, as well as to be together." This can best find expression if Russians can be with Russians or if they can be made to feel at one with Americans. Under the conditions prevailing in America, this social impulse does not find normal outlet with Russians and practically not at all with Americans. "A people can be judged and its career can be predicted from the character of its pleasures, with more accuracy than from any other data." [22] We have already seen that the Russian has a background of wholesome recreation in his homeland. His folksongs and native festivals far surpass in sociality our usual American pleasures. Here, the Russian can attend a moving picture play and gaze silently at what is usually an abnormal and frequently harmful exhibition purporting to be American life. [23] But this really does

[22] Giddings, *Democracy and Empire, op. cit.,* p. 243.
[23] In several cities and states in 1921 there has been an organized movement against the low quality of the moving pictures. New York State passed a moving picture censorship law. Michigan prohibits the exhibition of a crime, and Kalamazoo attempts to enforce the law. Things reached such a pass in Tulsa, Oklahoma,

not offer scope for the expression of the social impulse, it merely arouses the emotions.

Conclusion

It is, then, apparent that in most of these recreational activities, little contact is made with the good side of American life, although some of our foibles such as cheap "jazz" music and questionable moving pictures are foisted upon the Russian. We have seen that he usually lives in a cheap foreign district among a group using an alien language and having, in the main, different manners, customs, amusements, arts, and standards of living from the American. It is one of the striking achievements of our civilization that we do reach the foreign children to some extent, but we give them only the barest opportunity to secure something of our culture and well-being. We are content to leave their parents isolated in a foreign atmosphere, and in that environment the children are brought up. Some device ought to be utilized to bring these people into contact with good American influences.

The foreign-born Russian instead of growing more like-minded with Americans through the forces we have herein described has, too often, been growing still further unlike. There are few points of common stimulation, inter-stimulation and response

that after a campaign against the portrayal of crime in the motion pictures, one newspaper, the *Tulsa Tribune,* refused to accept all moving picture advertising.

between Americans and Russians to bring about re-semblance. In order to analyze still further the causes determining this differentiation, we shall next discuss the educational and religious social forces which surround the Russian Slav.

CHAPTER V

ORGANIZED SOCIAL FORCES: RELIGIOUS AND
EDUCATIONAL

The Russian Greek Orthodox Church

WE have already noted in Chapter II that representatives of the Russian branch of the Eastern Orthodox Church followed the Russian colonists to Alaska and California toward the end of the eighteenth and the beginning of the nineteenth centuries. As immigration to the United States increased, the number of churches and priests multiplied until in 1916 there were 169 churches with 99,681 members.[1] This membership includes all the men, women and children living in a parish who ever attend services; the majority are Ruthenians from Galicia, and not strictly Russian Slavs. The church is controlled by an archbishop who, until the revolution, was appointed by the Holy Synod in Russia. This Synod used $77,850 annually from the Tsar's treasury for the support of the mission in America; in addition, the Missionary Society of Russia donated $1,481.

The churches in America are divided into twenty-

[1] Bureau of the Census, *Religious Bodies, 1916* (Washington, 1919), part 2, p. 261.

seven districts supervised by superintendents appointed by the Archbishop. It is the custom in the Greek churches to hold religious services on Saturday evening and Sunday morning. Religious instruction is usually provided for the children, either on Saturday, or during the week after school hours. In 1916 there were 126 such schools with 150 officers and teachers and 6,739 students.[2] The instruction is carried on in the Russian language, and several priests frankly told the author that up to the revolution the attempt was made to keep the children loyal to the Tsar and to Russia. The chief subjects taught are: the Russian language, Russian history, Bible history, the catechism, prayers and church singing. Besides this, the church maintains a theological seminary, a girls' college, an immigrant home, a monastery which in 1916 contained 12 men, and an orphanage which in the same year supported about 55 children.

Affiliated with the Church is the Russian Orthodox Society of Mutual Aid, which was founded in 1895. Its aim is to spread and strengthen the Orthodox faith and church organization in America and to provide insurance for accident, sickness, and death besides aiding widows and orphans. It also maintains a weekly paper.[3] In April, 1920, the so-

[2] In 1920, when the author visited these schools, the priests testified that there had been a great falling off in attendance of children, due to the unpopularity of the church.

[3] Bureau of the Census, *Religious Bodies, 1916*, part 2, *op. cit.*, p. 260.

ciety had 188 Brotherhoods with 7,336 members, composed largely of workingmen. The largest number came from the borders of Hungary, the next largest from Russia. In the period from 1905 to 1918 inclusive, the society paid out for death benefits $677,787.85, for sick benefits $53,845, and gave in charity $164,013.03. In April, 1920, its total insurance liability was $5,304,500. Five-sixths of the membership was insured for either $500 or $1,000.[4] Besides this organization there is a rival mutual aid company, the Russian Brotherhood Society, which also enrolls many of the attendants of the Russian Orthodox Church. This society was organized in 1900 as the result of a split in the Ukranian People's Society. From the beginning it stood firmly on a nationalistic platform for Russia from first to last, refusing to be associated with any agitation in favor of an independent Ukraine.[5] In 1917 the Russian Slav membership was about 3,000 out of a total of over 12,000. Over half the men were insured for $600 and over one-third for $1,000, while over four-fifths of the women were insured for $300.[6] From its organization in 1900 to 1920, this society paid out over 1,850 death claims totalling over a million dollars. It is therefore apparent that these organizations have rendered

[4] Russian Orthodox Society of Mutual Aid, *Russians and Orthodox in North America* (Wilkesbarre, Pa., 1920), pp. 136-137 (tr. from Russian).

[5] E. I. Omeltchenko, *Russian-American Register* (N. Y., 1920), p. 214.

[6] Omeltchenko, *op. cit.,* p. 215.

service to the Russian workers in the emergencies of sickness and accident. But being distinctly Russian they have failed to give them an insight into American life.

Although these societies are democratically organized, the church as a whole, coming as it has out of the Russia of the Tsars, is quite the reverse. The Russian workmen give their savings for its support, yet have little or no voice in its management. In some cases the funds for church maintenance are deducted directly from their pay envelopes; for example, in Coaldale the coal companies deduct one-half a day's wage from each Russian worker every month and give it to the priest. His receipts from this source in 1919 were $14,917.78. The church there cost $200,000, so he claimed, having a debt of only $26,000 outstanding. Although these Russian workers are thus constrained to support the church, they yet have no power to elect their priests and the property stands in the name of the Archbishop at New York.

Following the revolution in Russia, many of the members became dissatisfied with the autocratic control which vested all the titles to the property in the name of the Archbishop. One instance occurred in Chicago when some of the congregation demanded an accounting of money contributed. Their demands finally became so insistent that the priest preached a sermon in which he said that the money belonged to the Lord and would be accounted for to him. This so enraged a portion of his listeners that they protested loudly in the midst of the service. The final result was the starting of an Independent Church which used many of the old ritual forms but the title to the property rested with the parishioners.[7] Much the same thing happened in the Russian Orthodox All Saints' Church in Detroit, organized in 1914. During 1918 there was a growing controversy among the members as to who should own the property. In November a new priest was sent to the congregation in spite of the objections of many. Finally, dissension became so general that in March, 1919, members of the church had a meeting at which a new board was elected, the majority being in sympathy with the democratic management, control and ownership of the church by the congregation. The old board refused to give over the property, and an independent church was formed. In 1920 there were independent churches in Chicago, Detroit, New York, Boston, Philadelphia, Brooklyn, Baltimore, Bayonne City, N. J., and Lawrence, Mass. These used the old forms and acknowledged the authority of the Patriarch in Russia, but would not submit to the authority of the acting head in America. Ordinarily these separate churches carry on a larger educational and social work than do the Orthodox ones.

The Orthodox Church has been still further weak-

[7] According to the testimony of several who had been in the congregation at that time.

ened by various unfortunate occurrences within its own organization. A suit was brought against the Archbishop and Consistory by seventeen priests, charging offenses ranging all the way from fraudulent handling of money to personal immorality.[8] This resulted in the court's appointing a Receiver.[9] Since the revolution the acting Archbishop has had fifteen lawsuits on his hands, five of them concerning the control of church property. United States customs officers also seized goods belonging to the church because, although they had been admitted free of duty into America, the church was now selling them. The autocratic character of the church was frankly admitted when the Archbishop declared that he was accountable to no one. He stated further that there was no necessity for keeping books, since the goods were sold if the customer had money, and if not were given away.[10] The powerful Orthodox Society of Mutual Aid attacked Archbishop Alexander in their paper and year-book on three grounds:[11]

1—That he had been intriguing to get his predecessor Evdokim out of America in order to seize control himself.

[8] Taken from an unprinted brief submitted in the legal proceedings, J. S. Kedrofsky against Archbishop and Consistory of the Russian Orthodox Greek Church, Supreme Court, New York County (1919).

[9] The order appointing Mr. Francis S. Bangs, Receiver, was made March 22, 1919, and was filed in the office of the Clerk of New York County, March 24, 1919.

[10] From the brief for the defense in answer to that of Kedrofsky in the suit against the Archbishop, *op cit.*

[11] Russian Orthodox Society of Mutual Aid, *op. cit.,* p. 59.

2—That in reality he favored an independent Ukraine.

3—That he had tried to break up the Orthodox Society of Mutual Aid.

All these facts, many of which were sensationally treated in the Russian press, strengthened the bad impression made. Many Russians, some of whom may have been previous supporters of the church, became deeply suspicious of its purpose and sincerity.

Before the revolution, when the church was more popular among the rank and file, it had been given, as we have noted, a yearly subsidy from Russia, and prayer was regularly made for the Tsar. It frankly tried to keep the people loyal to him, and to Russia, according to the testimony of priests to the author. The feeling of an educated Russian in Cleveland was, "The priests are simply the Tsar's officials." In 1920, three years after the revolution, a priest in Pennsylvania showed me into his study in which still hung pictures of Tsar Nicolas and the nobility. Another priest, himself, said that the church in America had always been used in the interest of the Tsar's government, and had often tried to make its parishioners dislike America that they might remain loyal to Russia.

In the *Russian Land,* a religious Russian newspaper, there appeared in 1916 a series of anti-American articles signed "Black Diamond." In the lawsuits brought by Father Kedrofsky it was charged that Archbishop Alexander was the author. While this is denied by the church authorities and probably justly so, it seems unfortunate that a religious periodical purporting to reflect the spirit of the Orthodox Church should have published such attacks on America. A sample is here given in order that the reader may gather something of the state of mind of the editor.[12]

SWEET LAND OF LIBERTY

All the factories are the selfsame ichor which poisons the worker's soul and body. Capital is a cruel master; workers are his slaves foredoomed to death. Each working day shortens the worker's life for a few months, saps the living juice out of him, dries out the heart, dampens the noblest aspirations of the soul; transforms a living man into a sort of machine, embitters the whole life. The ragged soul and body of the worker bring forth to the world half sick children, paralytic, idiotic—therefore the factory's poison kills not merely the unfortunate workers, but also whole generations. It kills invisibly, imperceptibly, in such a manner that the workers themselves—the voluntary slaves of capital—fail to see the whole frightfulness of their own situation. . . .

In Russia, more attention is paid to the man. There, they say: "Men are not cattle"; "Men are not made of iron"; "Work and rest." The mining of gold and silver and iron is called in our land "sing-sing work" (hard labor) which

---

[12] From no. 203 for Friday, August 26th. The translation is given in the main as presented in the brief of Kedrofsky, but has been checked over by the author with the newspaper article itself. Individual words may be translated differently, but the spirit of the article is correct.

is done by the most hopeless of criminals, not by thieves but by cut-throats—soul-killers or traitors to the State; whereas in America any work is sing-sing (hard labor), and the workers are galley slaves although they call themselves free citizens.

In contrast with this, the church has published many patriotic things; usually in its services there are prayers for the President of the United States and sometimes sermons on patriotic themes. On Sunday, October 26th, 1920, for instance, at the service in the cathedral in New York, the priest spoke on Theodore Roosevelt, and afterwards at the door blanks for the Roosevelt Memorial Association were handed out. Nevertheless, the church as a whole is frankly a Russian institution, giving the Russian little about America. Its priests, for the most part, do not even speak English.

The attitude of the ordinary workman toward the church is one of suspicion. Stephen Graham in his book, *With Poor Immigrants to America,* reported a Russian here as saying that the priests keep the immigrant down, that they like to have the immigrants drunk in order to get more money from them, and that it would be a good thing if the Orthodox churches were demolished and the priests sent to Europe. After the Bolshevik revolution the priests incurred enmity from many more by taking a partisan stand in the civil war. One in Cleveland gave out anti-Bolshevik propaganda and urged the men to sign up to fight with Kolchak. The church leaders, also, in many cases supported the owners of the businesses in which their parishioners worked. In Hartford, Father ——— told me that he knew of one priest who, in time of strike, received money from an employer to urge the men in his congregation to return to work. In Philadelphia the priest asserted that the Bethlehem Steel Co., at South Bethlehem, Pa., in 1918 forced each Russian workman to pay $1 a month to the Orthodox Church. Those who refused were discharged. He added, "If only all the companies would adopt this policy we would have no difficulty." It is only natural that the priests should strive to secure financial support from the companies which employ Russians. The following letter reveals the method adopted by one in Akron in 1918 and to some extent reveals his state of mind. The priests have testified to the author that they seldom meet with success in such appeals.

Mr. F. A. Seiberling, President,
The Goodyear Tire & Rubber Co.,
Akron, Ohio.

DEAR SIR:

Not less than three thousand of your employees are speaking the Russian language and still more than such were born in or belonged to the Russian Greek Orthodox Catholic Church.

True Christianity always makes a man better in all respects. One cares more for his family, is more earnest in his work, is less vulnerable to the poisonous teachings of some modern agitators trying to inoculate hate, envy and crime into those hearts of men where Christianity has planted love, respect, order and justice after long years of painstaking work.

The present conditions are particularly critical to the Russian workingmen who, without proper education and surrounded by new conditions of life, may become the adepts of some devilish doctrine, nourished in concealment by treacherous enemies of the United States. They may become infested with such doctrines unless the moral influence of their mother church will save them. We need a couple of thousand dollars to finish our task, but as I am most of the time on my missionary work, it will take a long time before I shall be able to pay the above money, unless a well meaning citizen, as you, with a broad understanding and sincere desire to improve our working community morally as well as materially, will contribute to the construction of this church, which no doubt is a great factor in the up-building of higher morals and better material conditions of this community.

As per custom of our church, we shall pray every Sunday for those who helped to build this temple of the Lord, and God will recompense you tenfold for what you will contribute to the benefit of his faithful worshipers.

Your sincere friend and humble servant of the Lord.

In Pennsylvania an Orthodox Father told the author that his predecessor secured funds to build a church by pledging the workmen that the money advanced would be paid back to them. Now he leaves and his successor is, of course, unable to repay the money.

All these things add to the hostility of the workmen against the church. One priest in Brooklyn estimated that 75 per cent of the Russians oppose the church. "Even if bread were offered to them free from a church," he said, "they would refuse. As long as a Russian is healthy, he does not need the church." That the masses from Russia have always distrusted the Orthodox Church and that this is the reason why such a large part of its membership is made up of Ruthenians, is the opinion of E. I. Omeltchenko,[18] who as member of the Extraordinary Russian Mission sent to the United States after the revolution by the Temporary Government, made a survey of the Russian colonies in America. If the church has always been unpopular among Russians, it is doubly unpopular now. In his investigations the author visited church after church, where there were only five or six in the audience during the services. The priests complained bitterly that contributions were exceedingly small. Joseph B. Polonsky, manager of the Russian Section of the Foreign Language Information Service of the American Red Cross, recently made a trip to the more important Russian colonies, going as far west as North Dakota. After visiting all the Orthodox churches he reported that the priests were preaching to only a mere handful; in consequence many asked him about securing other work for themselves.

In spite of these facts, individual churches are

[18] In a statement to the author.

popular and the Cathedral in New York is usually
well filled on a Sunday morning. It must not be
forgotten, moreover, that many of these Russian
priests are sincere men who are unselfishly trying to
serve. The writer became convinced that many are
really doing a splendid work for their parishioners.
Even if the Russian workman is distrustful of the
church, he is likely to attend on Easter and at
marriages. For funerals and christenings even the
skeptical feel the need of the church. The priests
are, at least, sharing the isolation of the mining
camps at meager salaries and are giving their
countrymen the opportunity of having beautiful
religious services.

The Protestant Church

The work of the Protestant Church on behalf of
the Russians is very small even in the aggregate.
The U. S. Census of Religious Bodies tells us that
all the Protestant denominations combined, not
counting the Greek Orthodox and the Roman
Catholic, have only fifteen churches exclusively Russian, with a total of only 811 members. In addition
there were ten churches with a mixed membership of
3947, which included a variety of other nationalities
besides Russian.[14] It must be remembered that
even these figures are likely to be somewhat
exaggerated, for a Russian pastor of one such

[14] Bureau of the Census, *Religious Bodies, 1916,* part 1, *op. cit.,*
pp. 78-82.

church told me that the number enrolled as members included many whose addresses the church no longer knew. Apart from any matter of membership, the Protestant Church does touch others who are not members. For example, the St. Paul's M. E. Church in Jersey City, N. J., permitted a group to organize in their own way and to hold meetings as they wished in the church rooms. They called themselves "The Russian Self-Educated Circle." Soon the number of members reached about sixty. They had an open forum every Saturday night following a lecture, and classes in English were held on Monday and Tuesday nights. Later, mathematics and civics were added. Voluntarily this group began to make contributions to the church expenses and finally several joined the church on their own initiative. Now, with entertainments and moving pictures added, this church has a group of about 300 Russians in its settlement work in Jersey City and 200 in Elizabethport. The Church of All Nations and the Labor Temple in New York City have also reached numbers of Russians who were not members. The Gary Chapel and Neighborhood House in Gary, Ind., have tried to help all the various nationalities, including the Russian. Eight national foreign societies hold meetings in the house. There are classes in English, boy scout meetings and religious services. Even making due allowance for all such work, what the Protestant Church is doing is almost negligible in comparison with the numbers involved, approximating two hundred thousand Russians in the United States. Moreover, much of the work is conducted by Russians in the Russian language, without any attempt to teach English. Among all the Russian churches listed in the United States Census, only two used the English language as well as the Russian in their services. For the most part they are conducted on a strict denominational basis, rigidly emphasizing certain dogmas. An analysis of fifty tracts printed by eight different organizations in Russian and collected by the Inter-Church World Movement showed that in general they were based on the literal divine inspiration theory of the Bible and used "the proof text" method. Fourteen were attempts to prove some disputed theological dogmas, such as the observance of the Sabbath on Saturday instead of Sunday. Considering all the phases of its activity, therefore, the influence of the Protestant Church in Americanizing the Russians is slight.

American Public and Private Agencies

The greatest assimilating agency that we have in America is the public school. Jane Addams says that the only service America is thoroughly equipped to offer the immigrant and his children is free education. When we consider that in 1910, according to the census, over one-fourth of the children in our schools were of foreign or of mixed parentage, we can realize something of the service that is being rendered the foreigner in this way.

Several private agencies, are however, trying to meet the needs of the alien. The social settlements invite the Russians along with other nationalities. One in New York City, for instance, offers its rooms for the use of Russian groups who have nowhere else to meet. It now has four such groups, and, as a result, several individuals have joined the English classes and other activities which the settlement maintains.[15] But the settlement reaches chiefly the women and children, and of these not many among the Russians.

The Y.M.C.A. in its industrial departments and among the foreign-born has frequently done good work for the Russians. The Brooklyn Association, for one, has organized an English class in Brownsville. This class has been popular and has already stimulated a number of the men to take out citizenship papers. Mr. Harvey Anderson and Mr. Thomas Cotton in New York, and Mr. Theodore G. Demberg in Philadelphia have also been active. They have organized lectures, classes, and information bureaus for the Russians, besides coöperating with other welfare agencies in the city.

The Y.W.C.A., through its International Institutes, serves the Russians in various ways. In Pittsburgh, for example, it has an information service with a paid Russian worker, and any who

[15] Daniels, *America via the Neighborhood* (N. Y., 1920), p. 227.

need advice or help can receive it there. Besides this, classes in English are conducted in the factory districts where the Russians live.

The Foreign Language Governmental Information Bureau organized by the Committee on Public Information of the Government and now affiliated with the Red Cross has been rendering notable service as a connecting link between the Government and the alien. At first it sent bulletins to the Russian papers giving material relating chiefly to the war; later it began to give general information to Russians. By interpreting our laws, it was the means of saving them thousands of dollars of income taxes wrongly collected. It has translated books on hygiene, technical works, histories of the United States, works on citizenship, and historical plays for the free use of the foreign language schools, churches and societies. Moreover, it has sent Russian lecturers to all parts of America who speak in Bolshevik clubs, workmen's halls and other meeting places on such subjects as American Ideals or Abraham Lincoln.

During and since the war, Americanization committees have had a mushroom growth. While there is no doubt that they have done a great deal for the foreigners, they have not touched the life of Russians as much as that of other nationalities. In illustration of this: an investigator of Russian conditions for a department of our Government says, "The Pittsburgh public school authorities are carrying on Americanization campaigns, aided by the Chamber of Commerce, which every so often invites the 'leaders' of the foreign-born to a dinner. As far as the Russians are concerned the results of this work are invisible." [16] Mr. George Creel, Head of the Committee on Public Information of the Government during the war says, "Americanization activities have largely been stupid when they were not malignant. . . . The sinister attempts of employers to identify Americanization with industrial submissiveness are with us to-day as in the past." [17] A Russian priest in Cleveland expressed his feelings about the Americanization work by saying, "If I came to Russia and they made me disown everything dear to me and swear I loved hard work in the factory and bad housing I would never become a Russian." Mr. Sibray, the United States Immigration Commissioner in Pittsburgh, says, "Our Americanization committees are largely a sham. On the average they think merely of getting the foreigner to take out citizenship papers and that is the last thing that ought to be done." A social organization in 1920 sent a Russian officer to make a study of the Russians in Cleveland and asked him to visit the Americanization committee because it has done notable work for many of the nationalities. In his written report, after questioning what the committee had done for the Russians, he said, "Almost none

[16] From a letter, of which the author has a copy.
[17] *Foreign Born,* Jan., 1920, p. 19.

of the Russians knew anything about America, Americanization committees, or the Y.M.C.A."

A quotation from one of the Russian papers is characteristic of the feeling of most of the Russians with whom the writer talked: "Many Americanization committees exist only on paper. They make much noise, praise themselves in the newspapers, but they do not do much good. . . . They mostly laugh about the poor foreigners. . . . If they want to help, they must come with love in their hearts." [18]

No doubt the Russians at the present time are difficult to reach because they have suffered from the fact that the public has associated them with the Bolsheviks in Russia. The Americanization committees are contending with a difficult problem and have naturally confined their efforts to the nationalities that responded most readily.

Government agencies such as the California Immigration Commission have done some constructive work in giving information to Russians and in forcing Americans to improve working conditions for their employees.[19] This commission has realized that one of the important tasks of all Americanization work is the education of the American employer in his responsibility toward the workman. One reason that American agencies fail to do more is that large numbers of the Russians are illiterate, and this fact is not sufficiently taken into considera-

[18] From *Pravda*, Sept. 30, 1919.
[19] Davis, *Immigration and Americanization, op. cit.*, pp. 440-473.

tion. The U. S. Immigration Commission in 1910 found that out of a total of 7,390 Russians interrogated, 29.5 per cent admitted that they could not read and write.[20] The illiterates among the Russians entering this country for the five years from 1910-1914, when the war stopped immigration, roughly averaged 35 per cent.[21] As the average Russian at the port of entry would probably claim that he was literate if he could read anything at all, these figures are probably low. If, then, over one-third of the Russians are illiterate it is not strange that they do not learn English, especially when it is realized that they are practically isolated from Americans and that they live, sleep and work together. Since an average of 35 per cent are illiterate and a much larger number can read but little in their own language, how can we expect them to keep up with a mixed class of various nationalities? In Mr. Cole's study in Chicago, out of 112 Russian workmen, 80 said they could speak some English, but only 12 claimed to be able to read it, and in the case of these 12 no test was made. The fact is that there have been few scientific attempts made to understand how to help the Russian learn English. As Professor Petrunkevitch of Yale says:

Although ostensibly for the benefit and instruction of uneducated and foreign workmen [the night schools] are, as

[20] U. S. Immigration Commission, *Abstracts of Reports,* vol. 1, table 77, pp. 438-442.

[21] Calculated from the U. S. Bureau of Immigration, *Annual Reports of the Commissioner-General,* table 7, pp. 20-21, 1910; pp. 20-21, 1911; pp. 74-75, 1912; pp. 46-47, 1913; pp. 42-43, 1914.

at present constituted, in reality of very little help. The Russian workman has first to learn English before he can understand instruction in other subjects; but even in this, he becomes quickly discouraged. He is a stranger to the teacher, who does not take into account his peculiar psychology. A few days, perhaps a few weeks of most strenuous work in the evening after the day's work at the factory, and the Russian workman gives up in despair.[22]

Russian Non-Political Organizations

In spite of the agencies we have listed, the foreign-born Russians in the aggregate are largely untouched. Probably more have been reached by the Foreign Language Information Service than by any other means, for in addition to other methods, it sends out information through the Russian press.

The Russians have a mass of organizations of the small non-political type in various parts of America. There are a few trade unions which are either Russian or else have Russian branches—for example, the Russian-Polish department of the Union of Cloakmakers, the Russian branch of the Union of Men's and Women's Garment Workers, the Society of Russian Bootmakers, and the Society for Russian Mechanics. All of these admit Russian Jews as well as other Russian nationalities.

There are also cultural-educational societies, of

[22] Petrunkevitch, Alexander, "The Russian Problem in the United States," *The Standard*, Feb., 1920, p. 176.

which, perhaps, the largest is *Nauka* (Science). This was organized in 1905 and had in 1918 six branches.[23] Besides paying a sick benefit of $5 a week and $200 in case of death, the society has a reading room and organizes lectures, concerts and socials. Other similar ones are *Znamenie* (The Sign), *Samo Obrazovanie* (The Society of Self-Education), *Prosvishenie* (Enlightenment), and the Society of Russian Citizens. In Boston and some other places there are branches of a Society of Mutual Aid for Russian Workers. It is their aim to have one member who will be expert on some one particular need of the Russian, such as: sending money to Russia, purchasing steamship tickets, employment, housing, and so forth. Since the organization is poor, all such activities have to be carried on voluntarily. The regulations of the society recognize the dangers involved and provide that no one so appointed shall have a secret arrangement with any company or agent whereby he makes a profit.

In the past few years a number of societies have sprung up which relate directly to the Russian revolution. Thus, in Los Angeles, there was formed a Society to Help Free Russia; in other places there were organizations for the sending home of political emigrants. While these sound very well as names, in practice most of them are very small and at

[23] Vilchur, M., *The Russians in America, op. cit.,* pp. 124-125 (tr. from the Russian).

best serve as centers providing a social rendezvous and an occasional lecture, but rarely affording any contacts with Americans or giving much information on America. Two Russian educational institutions are, however, doing extensive work. One is the Russian Collegiate Institute in New York City, which received a grant of $10,000 from the Carnegie Foundation and raised $6,000 from other sources. Its purpose is "to offer to Russian workmen within a small radius of New York City useful knowledge which will enable them to better their economic and social position." [24] All political subjects are forbidden and the school is open to all, whether pro- or anti-Bolshevik.

The institute is divided into three departments: (1) preparatory or night school, (2) academic, and (3) technical. The night school prepares the workmen for entrance into such institutions as Cooper Union. Instruction is given two hours every evening except Saturday and Sunday. The subjects taught are English, Russian, geography, history, arithmetic, algebra, trigonometry, physics and chemistry.

Besides these courses, the institute is carrying on lectures before larger groups than can attend the classes. Its secretary claims an average weekly attendance of 1,400 from January to May, 1921.

A similar school, called the Russian People's

[24] From an article by Alexander Petrunkevitch, the President of the Institute, in *The Standard*, Feb., 1920, *op. cit.*, pp. 177-178.

University, was started in Chicago with a foundation of $10,000 contributed by interested Russians. It has adopted also a non-political attitude and in May, 1919, had an enrolment of about eighty. The courses in agriculture proved to be the most popular since many Russians desire to prepare for such work in Russia. Undoubtedly these institutions are doing something toward giving the Russian a better understanding of America, but they exist in only two cities. Even taking into consideration all the societies mentioned, the Russian is relatively unorganized, as is shown in the 1917 survey of E. I. Omeltchenko, already mentioned. He concludes that in respect to organizations the real Russians have the least of all. "They are out of touch with every kind of cultural and educational influence both American and Russian." [25]

Russian Political Organizations

Before the author started visiting the Russian colonies, he secured lists of Russian socialistic, anarchistic, and radical clubs. The names and addresses included over 200. Probably the largest and most extensive of these was the Union of Russian Workers, which has branches in every large industrial center and in many small mining and manufacturing communities. It unites all the Russian workers affiliated with it, regardless of their

[25] Omeltchenko, E. I., *On the Question of the Organization of the Russian Colony* (N. Y., 1917), p. 5.   (*Cf.* footnote Preface, p. viii.)

trades, into one revolutionary organization, endorses direct action, and, in general, is sympathetic with anarchistic theories. Each branch is composed of not more than sixty members. It has no relation to other American organizations, although it is in friendly affiliation with some Russian anarchistic groups.[26] Its purpose is given in the agreement of the Federation of the Union of Russian Workers of the United States and Canada.[27]

THE FUNDAMENTAL PRINCIPLES OF THE FEDERATION

The present Society is divided into two opposing classes: on one side the unprovided laborers and peasants who have created the world's riches with their labor; on the other side the rich men who grabbed all those riches into their hands.

Many times has the unprovided class arisen against the parasitic rich and their trusty servant and defender, the Government, for the purpose of gaining full liberation from the yoke of capital and authority, but each time suffers defeat because it does not know clearly the ultimate purpose and the means whereby to gain it and becomes a tool in the hands of its enemies.

The strife between those classes is continuing also at the present time, and will be finished only when the working masses, organized into a class, will understand their true interest and will take possession by means of forceful revolution of all the wealth of the world.

[26] *Ibid.*, p. 6.
[27] Translation given to the author at the Detroit office of the United States Department of Justice.

Having accomplished such transposition, and having destroyed at the same time all the institutions of Government and authority, the unprovided classes will have to announce a society of free producers who will be anxious to satisfy the needs of every separate individual which later, in turn, will give to the society its labor and knowledge.

To reach our purpose, we, first of all, prove the necessity of creating a wide class of revolutionary organization of toilers, which, leading a direct fight with all the institutions of capital and authority, must teach the laboring class initiative and self-action in all its undertakings, developing within it in this manner a recognition of the necessity of the unavoidability of a Universal Strike—Social Revolution.

Organizing, therefore, into UNIONS OF RUSSIAN WORKERS, WE, as a part of the toilers of the whole world, will strive in all our future work that the principles underlying the Federation will always be a leading thread in the matter of organization of the wide masses of Russian Immigrants for the speediest liberation of Russia and of humanity.

In spite of these radical statements, the unions are in reality quite peaceful, according to E. I. Omeltchenko, and existed for seven years without molestation until U. S. Attorney General Palmer declared them illegal. They did circulate a surprising amount of radical literature, however, for the author found the following pamphlets in Russian on sale: [28]

"What is Anarchism?" by Novomirski.

[28] The titles are, of course, translations from the Russian, in which the pamphlets are printed.

"God and Government," by Mihael Bakunin.

"Manifesto of Anarchist-Communists," by Novomirski.

"Whom Does the Soldier Serve?" Anonymous.

"The Question of Communism," by A. Karelin.

"The Chicago Drama—First of May, 1886," Anonymous.

"The Moral Beginning of Anarchism," by Peter Kropotkin.

"The Speech of Matreni Presashuk before the Kiev War Tribunal the 19th of July, 1918."

It is unnecessary to quote from these for the titles and authorship show, for the most part, that they are radical. The pamphlet concerning the soldiers tries to prove that they simply serve the rich; that on the Chicago Drama describes America as a land where there are more hungry, more oppressed, more slaves than in any other land. It tells of "the shedding of the workers' blood" in Chicago by the militia, and says that up to the present time many thousands of people have lost their lives fighting for freedom in America, and that the laws are made simply to protect the power of the rich and private property.

One of the most dangerous is the Manifesto of Anarchist-Communists. In one place it says: "We may, therefore, formulate our tactics thus: By participating in the struggle of the working class, guiding it, and uninterruptedly widening and deepening that struggle, kindle and maintain the conflagration of civil war until we have torn up by the roots Capitalism and Government." These pamphlets, however, are circulated by only a few. Many Russians whom the author interviewed did not seem to be interested in the propaganda but rather in having a social club and in attending classes.

Besides this Union there are many branches of the Russian division of the Socialist Party. In affiliation with these are a number of "Societies for the Help of the Russian Revolution." In 1915 eighteen branches joined together in a federation representing 300 members, and by the fall of 1917 there were 29 branches with an active paying membership of 600. Following the revolution the activity of these branches increased to such an extent that in 1919 there were 150 branches and over 12,000 members.[29] Moreover, a radical element that did not believe in parliamentary procedure began to agitate in favor of direct action. Before long the entire socialist party of Russians had accepted this position. There were three chief reasons: [29a]

(a) The vast increase of new members,
(b) Allied intervention in Russia,
(c) Dislike of Denikine and Kolchak, the leaders in the civil war against the Bolsheviks.

Many Russian socialists even plotted to overthrow the conservative leaders of the American party, but were thwarted when the executive committee threw out all non-American citizens. As a result of this

[29] Omeltchenko, *Russian-American Register, 1920, op. cit.,* p. 232.
[29a] *Ibid,* p. 232.

action, the Russian socialists, together with radicals from other groups, held a congress toward the end of 1919, which resulted in the formation of the American Communist party. A few breaking away from the others joined the American Communist Labor Party. *Pravda* (Truth) with a circulation of between three and four thousand was one periodical which supported their position.[30] This Communist Party also circulated considerable radical propaganda and in 1920 wholesale arrests of Russians followed. The radical Russian papers, *Pravda* and *Novy Mir,* were suppressed.[31]

In spite of these facts concerning the activities of the central organization, many of the socialist clubs visited by the author appeared to cater merely to the social impulse of the Russian. As is usually the case where some definite group activity arises, whether it be in connection with a saloon or whether it be a Communist club, some useful things were accomplished. For example, in New York City during the spring of 1918, 23 Russian organizations joined together to form a "soviet," [32] with headquarters at 133 East 15th Street.[33] The chief

[30] *Ibid.,* p. 233.
[31] Although not used as authority in this study, the Report of the Joint Legislative Committee Investigating Seditious Activities, *Revolutionary Radicalism* (Albany, 1920), in Chaps. v and vi pp. 739-818, treats of the formation of the Communist parties.
[32] A *soviet* is a council made up of the representatives of various organizations or professions.
[33] Some disbanded, others dropped out, and in 1919 the secretary said there were only thirteen left. The principal ones were: The Federation of Russian Workers, The Society of Russian Peasants,

feature of the activities in the building was the Soviet School. According to the secretary it was started by placing advertisements in the Russian papers and by holding large meetings and urging enrolment. By this means, in 1919, over 300 paid students were secured, and there were more applicants than there was room. Russian and English classes were started first, and later automobile and electrical classes, courses in algebra, history, astronomy and agriculture. If ten students desired some new course, the management arranged for it. If even a single individual left on the ground that the teacher was not satisfactory, a committee was appointed to investigate. Each student paid ten cents an hour for his class and each teacher received a dollar and a half. While undoubtedly considerable propaganda was circulated, the majority of the classes were in subjects which, by their nature, are not easily used for that purpose.

In Boston the author visited a club on Dec. 14, 1919. Hanging on the wall was a certificate of incorporation which read:

Mutual Aid Association of Workmen from Russia for the purpose of paying death or funeral benefits not exceeding two hundred dollars, and disability benefits not exceeding ten dollars per week. The association shall maintain a library and conduct lectures for the purpose of educating its members and also assist them in raising the standard of

The Society of Dock Workers, and two anarchistic groups publishing *Bread and Freedom* and *The Workman and Peasant.*

their living. The membership is limited to persons of Russian birth and descent.

The charter was granted by the State of Massachusetts on Dec. 6, 1915.

On the walls were pictures of all the Russian revolutionary leaders, Gorky, Lenin, Trotsky and others, and a certificate of membership in the Communist Party hung on the wall. The club had both men and women members. Classes in Russian and arithmetic met nightly and all the leading Russian daily newspapers were accessible. A buffet which served soft drinks actually paid for the rent of the room, which was twenty dollars a month. The club also maintained a school for the children of members which met three times a week. As far as one could judge, although the club included political elements, it also met a legitimate social and educational need, and to that extent was constructive. After listening for hours to study classes in the various Communist clubs, one could but admit that they do attempt to teach their own members. They also have merit in that they do not go over the heads of the illiterate workers. Still, such clubs also have lectures on Communism and Bolshevism, and there is little doubt that part of the propaganda work then going on in the club just described was directed against our political system and American ideals.

In addition to these groups the representative of

the Soviet Government, Mr. Martens, formed a
Technical Department of his Soviet Bureau. Its
purpose was to organize and register all the technical, industrial and professional strength of the
Russian colony in America to aid in building Russia
into a Communistic Socialistic Republic.[34] As was
testified to in the deportation hearing of Mr.
Martens: "This section has organized, throughout
all America, associations for technical assistance to
Soviet Russia, which now number more than ten
thousand members." [35] The societies which were
organized plan to send not only workers, but also
certain branches of production as a unit, with both
machinery and workmen. The popularity of the
plan and the extent of sympathy which exists toward
Soviet Russia is attested by the fact that it was
possible to secure 10,000 volunteers.

In spite of all that can be said in favor of these
educational programs, they are Russian in their
make-up and scope and certainly do not, in the main,
make the Russian love America or her institutions,
nor do they provide contacts with them. There may
be a few Russians who can say, as did one who wrote
to a government bureau, "The American socialists
helped me to love America. Then I understood
that America is not only composed of capitalists and

[34] Circular on "Technical Department of the Soviet Bureau in
America," published by the representative of the Russian Socialistic
Federated Soviet Republic in America.
[35] Brief on behalf of Mr. Martens argued before the Department
of Labor in 1921 (New York), p. 48.

bourgeois. Many great inventors were Americans."
But they seem to be rare. For the majority, such
clubs, while fulfilling a perfectly proper and natural
educational and social function, actually do stimulate
distrust of our government and her institutions.

The Russian and American Press

The newspapers and journals printed in Russian
in the United States have had a long and checkered
career. The first to be published was the *Alaska
Herald,* a bi-lingual semi-monthly periodical in
Russian and English. The English material was
arranged to interest Americans, and treated phases
of the political and social life of Russia. The
remainder gave items interesting to the Russians
about American life and laws, or about the Russian
colonies in Alaska and San Francisco. It was not
until 1889 that another periodical, the *Sign,* a
weekly, was issued; this lasted less than a year. From
that time on, there has been a constant appearance
and disappearance of periodicals and newspapers
M. Vilchur [36] lists 52 others, of which 18 were
discontinued during the first year of publication, 12
during the second year, 7 during the third year;
only 5 are now published in 1921. Of these five the
oldest started in 1902.

At present there are four Russian dailies published
in the United States. A fifth, the *Novi Mir* (The
New World) was suppressed by the Government in

[36] Vilchur, *The Russians in America, op. cit.,* pp. 114-117.

1920 because it was affiliated with the Communist Party in America. The I.W.W. weekly in Chicago, however, has been permitted to appear regularly, and is sent through the mail.

The history of the *Novi Mir* is worth recording, as showing how politics enter into the management, and so into the news given to the Russian readers. The *Novi Mir* was founded in 1911 by the Russian Socialist Publishing Association and represented the Social Democrats or Mensheviks, as the party is termed in Russia. The editorial board was elected by the 300 Russian members of the Socialist Publishing Association. At first the entire nine members of the board of management were Mensheviks. Gradually, after the paper became prosperous, the original 300 members dropped away until there were only 75 who remained active. Now, under the rules of the Association, anyone who had been a member of the Socialist Party for six months could join by paying one dollar. The Russian Bolshevik sympathizers decided to secure control of the paper. They persuaded Buharin and Chuduafsky, both Bolsheviks, to come from Sweden in 1916 with the intent of placing them on the editorial staff. Under the rules of the management no one could get more than $15 in this capacity and the result was a dearth of good writers, so that it was easy to secure the positions for these able writers. Every month the Bolsheviks brought in new members to the Association

until they had secured a majority vote and won
control, whereupon all the Menshevik members
of the board resigned.[37] Leon Trotsky was on the
staff from Jan. 15, 1917, to March 27, 1917. In
1916 the Association, because it was opposed to
war, passed a resolution refusing the acceptance of
war loan advertisements. In October, 1917, the
second class mailing privilege was withdrawn by the
post office department. In November, 1917, the
paper was excluded from circulation in the United
Kingdom. In 1918 many copies of the paper were
held by the postal authorities; in the second half
of July, out of fourteen issues printed, ten were so
withheld. By August 12, 1918, thirty-seven issues
of the paper had been declared non-mailable under
the Espionage Act. On August 15th a disloyalty
order was issued, denying the paper the privilege of
receiving mail. In 1920 the paper was raided by
agents of the Lusk committee and its printing presses
were damaged; since then it has been closed. In
1918 the editor-in-chief was Gregory Weinstein,
who made the following statement regarding the
paper,[38] "*Novi Mir* is a revolutionary Socialistic
organ, supporting the Soviet government of Russia.
There is no connection between our party and the
I.W.W. Some of our aims may be similar, but we
do not work together. *Novi Mir* was excluded from

[37] According to Alex. Gumberg, a member of the Menshevik
staff, in a statement to the author.
[38] From an unpublished statement as given to a representative
of the Carnegie Foundation.

the mails here because we republished in our columns an article from the Hearst paper, the Washington *Times,* which said that the money to carry on the war should be raised by taxing capital." He claimed for the paper a circulation of 8,000.

Two of the four other dailies, the *Novoye Russkoye Slovo* and the *Russky Golos* are published daily, including Sunday, while the *Americanskiya Izvestia* and *Svobodnaya Russiya* do not appear on Sunday. Ayer's *American Annual* for 1921 gives the circulation for *Novoye Russkoye Slovo* as 32,256 (P. O. statement) and the *Russky Golos* as 35,143 (published statement).[39] The names of the other two papers are not given at all. Joseph B. Polonsky, already referred to as Manager of the Russian section of the Foreign Language Information Service of the American Red Cross, stated that the sworn and published statements were worthless and his testimony was corroborated by Mr. Vilchur, one time editor of the *Russkoye Slovo.* In the opinion of Mr. Polonsky, instead of 32,000, the *Novoye Russkoye Slovo* had a circulation of 10,000 and the *Russky Golos* about 15,000. He thought the *Amerikanskiya Izvestia* had a circulation of 3,000 and the *Svobodnaya Russiya* 3,000. As for the I.W.W. paper, *The Golos Trushenka,* instead of 6,000 claimed by the management, he thought no more than 700 copies were sold. It must be remembered

---

[39] Ayer, N. W., *American Newspaper Annual and Directory,* 1921 (Philadelphia), p. 1305.

in considering such figures that these papers circulate among Jews as well as the Slavs, with whom we are primarily concerned.

Besides the papers already named, there are two brotherhood publications which go to all the members of their respective organizations. *Svyet,* the organ of the Russian Orthodox Mutual Aid Society, is a weekly, and *Pravda,* the organ of the Russian Brotherhood organization, is a semi-weekly. The sworn statement of circulation of *Pravda* is 10,200,[40] but only 3,000 reach Russians.[41] *Svyet* has a sworn circulation of 7,000,[40] but the great majority are Karpatho-Russians.[42] Neither paper has much influence among the Russian colony, according to Mr. Polonsky. The Inter-Racial Council, after using the advertising columns of these two papers, says: "Experience has shown us that these papers have very little effect on molding the opinion of their readers." Most of the readers of the Brotherhood papers also have access to the Russian dailies. In view of the large circulation of the latter, and their presence in every Russian club and library, and since they were regarded by all the Russians with whom the writer has talked as the most influential, the author has subjected the four dailies to a special analysis, for the numbers from Jan. 15 to 21, 1921—a single week. This gives at least indicative results, since the papers' general make-up

[40] *Ibid., op. cit.,* p. 1305.
[41] Omeltchenko, *Russian-American Register, op. cit.,* p. 214.
[42] *Ibid.,* p. 212.

and the character of the articles are fairly uniform from week to week. Two of the newspapers were examined, both before and after the date selected, and no particular change in the character of the news from that of the week selected was noted, nor was there any special event in that week, which would give undue weight to one class of items. The purpose of this classification was primarily to discover how much space was devoted to America and her institutions. With this in view, the main classifications were: A—News Concerning Foreign Countries, B—News Distinctly American, C—News Relating Directly to the Activities of Russians in America, D—Topics Non-Classifiable as Strictly American, Russian, or Foreign. The editorials were placed in a class by themselves and were analyzed separately. No attempt was made to separate news from opinion. Many articles were a clever admixture of both.

Each of the main headings was further subdivided and a considerable number of items were classified as to whether they were distinctly favorable, distinctly unfavorable, or indifferent to the subject heading. After reading the classification given below, the method should be clear to the reader, but a few concrete illustrations may be an added help. For example, when one newspaper said a law was reactionary, this was considered unfavorable to the American Government. On the other hand, an item reporting the Senate as considering the passage of a resolution freeing political prisoners was considered indifferent. The term American "imperialist" was included with that of employers and capitalists because as used it apparently referred to business men interested in foreign trade. Under the heading, Unfavorable to the Methods of American Educational, Religious, or Welfare Institutions, were listed the attacks against the American public school, the Red Cross and the Relief Administration. Items relating to American institutions or achievements in general, such as an account of the development of agricultural machinery, was placed under the head "B-9, Other News About America."

The writer realizes that the classification of material as "favorable" or "unfavorable" and "indifferent" is open to the objection that it is subjective. Nevertheless, most articles by their tone or contents indicate rather distinctly whether they are hostile to American institutions or whether their effect would be to promote good will toward America. When there was doubt about an item, it was classified as indifferent. Some of the material which would be considered unfavorable to America by many Russian readers was purposely not included as such; for example, such items as: the discharge of a teacher in Buffalo for belonging to a radical party, the policing of the city against reds, the reduction of wages by an employer. On the other hand, items such as: U. S. Attorney General Palmer's action in arresting Russians reported illegal, the killing of a striker by a United States soldier and "the terrorizing of the countryside by soldiers" were considered as unfavorable material because of the distinctly hostile tone of the articles. Although a large aggregate of unfavorable material was found, it must be remembered that the tabulation was made while there was still considerable feeling over the Russian Revolution. It is possible that the results would have been quite different two years later. The classification follows for the four papers, showing the amount of space in newspaper column inches: [43]

A. News Concerning Foreign Countries

	Golos	Slovo	Izvestia	Russiya
1. Relating to Soviet Russia......	744	1,009	522	549
2. Relating to Other Countries....	715	408	319	534
Total Foreign Countries....	1,459	1,417	841	1,083

B. News Distinctly Relating to America or Americans

	Golos	Slovo	Izvestia	Russiya
1. American Government:				
Distinctly favorable..........	0	0	0	0
Distinctly unfavorable........	58	49	135	124
Indifferent	25	74	50	24
2. American History:				
Distinctly favorable to America	0	44	0	0
Distinctly unfavorable........	0	24	0	0
Indifferent	0	0	0	0
3. American Political Parties.....	0	3	0	0
4. American "Imperialists," Employers or Capitalists:				
Distinctly favorable to them..	0	0	0	0
Distinctly unfavorable.......	124	35	75	97
Indifferent	27	0	22	33
5. Accidents in Industry..........	0	9	0	0
6. Strikes and Labor Unions:				
Distinctly favorable to them..	0	0	0	0

[43] Width of columns was two and one-quarter inches. Headings were included.

	Golos	*Slovo*	*Izvestia*	*Russiya*
Distinctly unfavorable to conservative unions...........	0	49	0	0
Indifferent to them...........	55	31	29	40
7. The American Press:				
Distinctly favorable to some paper	0	0	0	0
Distinctly unfavorable........	0	7	6	0
Indifferent	0	0	0	0
8. American Educational, Religious or Welfare Institutions:				
Distinctly favorable to their Methods	0	0	0	0
Distinctly unfavorable........	0	0	18	31
Indifferent	2	3	10	0
9. Other News About America:				
Distinctly favorable to America	0	0	0	0
Distinctly unfavorable	0	14	28	29
All other....................	11	34	72	6
Total Distinctly Favorable.....	0	44	0	0
Total Distinctly Unfavorable...	182	178	272	281
Total Indifferent	120	154	173	103
Grand Total About America	302	376	445	384

C. NEWS DISTINCTLY RELATING TO THE ACTIVITIES OF

RUSSIANS IN AMERICA

	Golos	*Slovo*	*Izvestia*	*Russiya*
1. Russian Communism, Socialism or I. W. W.'ism in America (including items on political prisoners and those deported):				
Distinctly favorable to such forms of radicalism.......	20	0	247	45
Distinctly unfavorable........	0	0	0	0
Indifferent	19	22	100	5
2. Russian Literature or Education for Russians in America...	126	172	299	47
3. Religion	60	0	23	22
4. Recreation	60	219	96	5
5. Coöperatives	9	2	4	0
6. Other Russian Societies........	19	65	31	6
7. Russian Colonies in General....	37	0	283	4
Total	350	480	1,083	134

D. NEWS NOT CLASSIFIED AS STRICTLY AMERICAN, RUSSIAN OR FOREIGN

	Golos	*Slovo*	*Izvestia*	*Russiya*
1. Editorials (classified and analyzed later)	126	182	212	192
2. Poems, Stories and Anecdotes..	164	245	125	160
3. Crime	15	124	11	52
4. Remaining Items..............	196	170	20	13
Total	491	721	368	417
Grand Total for the Week.	2,602	2,994	2,737	2,018

The large total of unfavorable material is significant. In any American newspaper there would, no doubt, be items which would be so classified, but there would also be compensating favorable articles which in the aggregate would far outweigh the others. In all four newspapers the author found only forty-four inches of space which seemed to him distinctly favorable to America, while 913 were distinctly unfavorable. Even if the evaluation of the items given above is disregarded, the amount of space given to the various subjects is significant.

In the *Golos and Russiya,* over one-half of all the items are devoted to foreign countries and over one-quarter to Soviet Russia. In the *Slovo* over one-third of the space was filled with material relating to Soviet Russia and nearly half to foreign countries, while the *Izvestia,* which gives the least space of all to foreign affairs, devotes nearly one-third of the paper to them. To things American, in the *Golos,* there was only a total of 302 inches of space, and 206 inches of this were devoted to items about imperialists, capitalists, employers, strikes,

and labor unions—all topics likely to give a foreign
worker an unfavorable impression. In the *Slovo,*
376 inches of space were found relating to America,
but about one-third were on these same subjects,
and 178 inches of space seemed to the writer of the
present monograph to be unfavorable to America
in the sense primarily discussed. The *Izvestia* and
Russiya had a slightly larger amount of space
devoted to American items, but their aggregate of
unfavorable material was also greater by nearly
200 inches. None of the papers had anything of
importance about our American newspapers, but
what seemed far more unfortunate was the dearth
of information about American educational, religious or welfare institutions. In the news of the
activities of Russians in America considerable
attention was turned to Russian education, partly,
as was stated, for the purpose of stimulating the
reader to be ready to return to Soviet Russia when
it was possible to do so. But not a single item
mentioned such a thing as classes in English. There
was considerable story material, which did not seem
to have particular educational value. All the papers
are to be commended in having little or no space
advertising crime, and even the *Slovo,* which had
over double that in any of the others, gave it only
124 inches.

Besides the above classification of all the news, an
analysis of the editorials as to content and space
is an indication of the policy of the papers. This

analysis follows for each newspaper separately, with the translation of the heading in quotation marks and a condensed indication of the character of the editorial.[44]

THE RUSSKY GOLOS

1. "An Elderly Man Joins the Ranks of the   14 inches
   Communists"
   Applauds Anatole France for his decision.

2. "Keeper of the Public Order"   14   "
   About the corruption of our police force in the cities. One sentence reads, "Bribe-taking, that disease of the American police, is similar to the same malady under the old Tsar's order with this difference, that there it permeated all through from top to bottom, while with the American police it is rare among the rank and file but occurs at the top."

3. "Bakhmeteff Goes to Paris"   10   "
   Harding and the new administration must demand an accounting from Bakhmeteff for the American money he has spent.

4. "Echoes of Wrangel"   18   "
   Scathing attack on France for helping Wrangel against Soviet Russia.

5. "'If the Child Were Not Afraid, He   30   "
   Would Not Cry'"

[44] The translations given are only roughly made in the sense that individual words may have been loosely rendered, but the sentences as a whole express the spirit of the Russian text.

The Soviets are no longer afraid; hence
the capitalists all over the world have
given up using the phrase "the impending
fall of Soviet Russia."

6. "The Polish Nobility and the Polish Sol-   16 inches
     diers"
   The Polish nobility deceived the workers
   into fighting Russia. Now the workers
   pay for it with hunger and defeat.

7. "Major Allen Astonished"   8   "
   The Red Cross now admits that ninety
   per cent of the parents of the children
   sent to Soviet Russia are still alive.

8. "The Next Step—for the Americans"   16   "
   On the departure of the Soviet Bureau,
   "Soviet Russia has done everything she
   could to open trade and make peace with
   America; the next step rests with Amer-
   ica."

NOVOYE RUSSKOYE SLOVO

1. "What Will the State Department Admit?"   8   "
   Attacks the Department on its record regarding Russia. One sentence reads, "It
   is certainly astonishing that serious people, government people, wish after this to
   make the public believe that America has
   been faithful in her relationships to Russia."

2. "Again 'Constitutional Assembly'"   16   "
   Attacks as counter-revolutionary the so-
   called "Constitutional Assembly" of

Kerensky and Milyukov which is meeting in Paris.

3. "Five Months"   8 inches
Congratulates the *Novoye Russkoye Slovo* on the fifth month of the new management of the paper.

4. "The Question of Russia in the Senate"   12   "
Endorses Senator France's resolution favoring trade with Russia and states that responsible representatives of the Russians in America should be heard in the Senate Committee.

5. "Protection Against Disorderly Conduct"   12   "
Criticizes a man for attacking the Soviet régime. The blockade has made the facts difficult to obtain; a better protection against radicalism would be cultural propaganda.

6. "Minister Briand"   10   "
His attitude toward Russia.

7. "The Staff of the 'Workers'' Paper"   24   "
Attacks the *Amerikanskiya Izvestia*.

8. "The Senate Considers Bakhmeteff's Millions"   24   "
Says the Russian colony and part of the Russian press can give the Senate interesting information about the use by Bakhmeteff of the American people's dollars.

9. "How You Are Trusted, Comrade-Workers"   18   "
Attacks the other paper for not using

union labor. Says the condition of laborers in America is "inhuman."

10. "The Resolution of Senator Johnson About   30 inches
Siberia"
Concerning American intervention in
Siberia; one sentence reads, "Let there be
light in the dark corners of American
politics, in the matter that served the
Japanese imperialists and not one of the
American or Russian people."

11. "The Departure of the Soviet Bureau"   20   "
One sentence reads, "If it were possible
for the Russian colony to express its real
feeling they would have given Martens
an ovation."

AMERIKANSKIYA IZVESTIA

1. "Reaction in France Grows"   25   "
The French Government now declares the
General Confederation of Labor illegal,
although the Confederation has previ-
ously expelled all the revolutionary element.

2. "The Decay of the Austrian Government"   11   "
Austria is bankrupt.

3. "The Uniting of Russian 'Democracy'"   22   "
Attacks the "counter revolutionary" Russian leaders meeting in Paris in the name
of democracy.

4. "The Two Revolutionary Groups in Italy"   10   "
The workers who actually seize the factories are far better than those who
merely talk revolution.

5. "Communication with Vienna Broken"   18 inches
There is a rumor that Vienna is in the
hands of the workers. Since they are in-
ternationalists this will be advantageous.

6. "America on the Eve of a Mighty Strike"   21   "
Three millions are out of work. The
textile workers will fight against wage re-
ductions, the A. F. of L. against the open
shop. The workers demand trade with
Russia. The strike is the real weapon,
the employers the real enemy.

7. "Ambassador Bakhmeteff and the Scandal   24   "
at Washington"
Senator Norris demands an accounting
of the money advanced to Bakhmeteff by
the government. One sentence reads,
"The advance cost the Russian people
many lives, much blood."

8. "France 'Draws Out' the Reds"   10   "
France is arresting all "reds," among
them some Americans. One sentence
reads, "There are 'reds' who are not Russians. All workers are 'reds' in the sense
of being revolutionists."

9. "Wrangel's Soldiers Conspire"   21   "
Now at last his soldiers understand the
truth of the revolution and refuse to
fight against the Bolsheviks.

10. "The Moscow International and the Break-   12   "
up of the Socialist Parties"
The Moscow International has divided
the Socialist ocean in two.

11. "The Rejected Russians with Their Fami-   38   "

lies Leaving the Borders of the United
States To-morrow"

A stinging editorial against Attorney
General Palmer, the United States, and
the capitalists. In speaking of what the
Russian immigrant finds here, it says,
"Instead of happiness—a dried up piece
of bread, the sweat shop and the dark
labor of the galley slave, instead of peace
—perpetual ordering about, interference,
and in the end deportation—that is the
fate of the Russian worker and peasant
in America."

SVOBODNAYA RUSSIYA

1. "Does Russia Wish to Fight?" 26 inches
   Russia has always desired peace but
   propagandists and counter-revolutionists
   continually spread lies and prevent it.
2. "Bankrupt Austria" 10 "
   The Allies laid such a heavy indemnity
   on her that she has neither bread nor
   money.
3. "The Labor War in France" 16 "
   France has ordered the General Federation of Labor to disband, but the only
   result has been a labor war.
4. "An Unsuccessful Adventure" 14 "
   Poland is criticized for attempting to
   seize Vilna and Grodna.
5. "Russia Still in Disgrace" 20 "

America preaches humanity, justice, and democracy but does not practice these principles toward Russia. "In the parts of Russia under the control of the White Guard, America spends 4,400,000 dollars but in Soviet Russia, nothing."

6. "Industrial America and Russia"   16 inches
   There should be trade between America and Russia.

7. "Unemployment in England"   18   "
   England is condemned for wasting her efforts on Ireland and India when she has a million unemployed.

8. "A Summons to Disarmament"   18   "
   General Bliss and Lloyd George are among those who urge disarmament, but it remains talk and not action. In the meanwhile, the harsh peace points towards war.

9. "Afraid of Russia's Being Recognized"   20   "
   Russian counter-revolutionists urge intervention because they fear recognition.

10. "Discord between the Allies"   19   "
   France and England disagree over Turkey, Germany, and Russia. Some are benefiting because of this, the worst elements in Turkey, for instance.

11. "Again the White Guards"   15   "
   Internal and external foes fall on Russia, yet when she arms to meet the attack, the White Guards cry, "Russia is militaristic."

In the *Golos*, every single editorial except one within the week examined related directly or indirectly to Soviet Russia and that one was a discussion of the corruption connected with municipal police in America. In the *Slovo* every editorial related to Soviet Russia except three, which dealt with a rival newspaper. In the *Izvestia* every editorial except three dealt with conditions in foreign countries. Of the three exceptions, one condemned America, another urged the strike as the only real weapon of the workers, and the third accused the United States of advancing money, which action resulted in the loss of many Russian lives. In the *Russiya*, besides an editorial stating that the world is more likely to get war than disarmament, only two dealt with America. One of these urged trade between Soviet Russia and America, the other accused America of hypocrisy in preaching humanity and not helping Soviet Russia.

If the editorials are any criterion of the policy of the paper, none of these newspapers gives its readers much that is favorable to America, while all give some space to that which is unfavorable. Part of this may be due to the fact that revolutionists who have been driven out from a Tsar's despotism have often become influential in the policy of the Russian press in this country. Moreover, the content of the newspapers is largely devoted to Russia and Russians. It seems only natural that this should be so, for like individuals are interested

in like things. Their newspapers are mechanisms
for the dissemination of information interesting to
a particular group who differ in language, traditions,
and experience from Americans. Their support
comes from aliens who are Russians, out of touch
with the best of America, and it is to be expected
that they would discuss the life of Russians in
America, and the condition of the homeland. The
material presented about Soviet Russia is decidedly
favorable to the Bolsheviks. The Russian immigrants in America know from personal experience
something of the tyrannous character of the Tsar's
government, and from what they read in their
papers might well think the Bolshevik government
good. This makes the treatment of Bolshevism by
our American press stand out in striking contrast.
Comparatively few Russians are able to read American papers, but most of them have heard that the
attitude which is taken therein toward Soviet Russia
is hostile.

Summary

In this chapter we have seen that the organized
religious and educational forces which surround the
Russian Slav are largely foreign and un-American.
The Greek Orthodox Church came to this country
during the reign of the Tsar, and was aided by the
Tsar's money. At best it is a Russian influence,
binding its adherents to the old religious ceremonials
and retaining the mother-tongue. Following the

revolution many were alienated from its support because it failed to endorse the revolution enthusiastically. The work of the American Protestant Church with this nationality is slight and is along denominational and theological lines rather than social. American public and private agencies are striving to help the Russian, together with other foreign groups, but the magnitude of the problem of all the varied foreign-born has prevented them from reaching the great majority of Slavs. The barrier of illiteracy, and one of the most difficult European languages, has made a concentration on other nationalities the easiest course. The organizations which the Russians themselves have created are more potent, but they are largely radical and nationalistic. The Russian press in America prints little about America and some of what it does print is distinctly antagonistic to our government and institutions. As was found in regard to other conditions, the educational and religious opportunities open to Russians afford little chance for contacts with American life.

CHAPTER VI

Legislation

UNDER usual circumstances the ordinary Russian in America does not come into contact with our government directly, except through the police and the law courts. He is nevertheless markedly affected by certain legislation. The prohibition amendment makes it difficult for him to patronize the saloons. In the towns there may be none, in the cities illegal resorts may be open but are liable to be raided; moreover, the liquor is expensive. Incidentally the constant violation of the law which he sees going on everywhere cannot but weaken his sense of respect for all legislative enactments. This may be augmented by violations of ordinances against gambling, or even expectoration. If he reflects on the matter, it must seem strange to the Russian that in Pennsylvania a Sunday baseball game is illegal but that there is no prohibition of the seven-day week in the steel mill. A Russian priest made the comment that the Bible forbids work on the Sabbath but says nothing against base-ball.

Although the prohibition law touches many Russians, they realize that it applies to everyone. It is not discriminatory legislation. There are a number of state laws, however, which the Russian feels to be particularly directed against foreigners and his tendency is to overestimate their effect on himself. Many of these bills are passed for the commendable purpose of either compelling him to learn English or of stimulating him to take out citizenship papers, and may be necessary and just. On the other hand, enforcement of such legislation is difficult in most cases, and the foreigner who is arrested for failing to comply, is likely to feel unjustly treated. To cite a number of such enactments:

Kansas: Unless the alien has filed a declaration of intention to become a citizen, his property shall escheat to the state, in the event of his death.[1]

Massachusetts: Applicants for admission as attorneys at law must be citizens of the United States.[2]

Michigan: Persons not citizens can teach in the public schools only if they have filed their intention of becoming citizens.[3]

Nebraska: All public meetings—political meetings or conventions, the purpose and object of which are the consideration and discussion of political or non-political subjects of general interest, or relating to the well-being of any class or organization—shall be conducted in the English

---

[1] *Laws of Kansas 1921,* ch. 185, p. 278.
[2] Letter from the Department of Education of Massachusetts to the author cites *General Laws of Massachusetts,* ch. 221, sec. 37.
[3] State of Michigan, *General School Law* (1919), Act 220, p. 111.

language exclusively; providing the provisions of this Act shall not apply to meetings or conventions held for the purpose of religious teachings, instruction or worship, or lodge organizations.[4]

Aliens are prohibited from holding any public office in the state.[5]

Aliens may not teach in any public, private, or parochial school.[6]

It is illegal for aliens to own, keep, or have firearms in their possession.[7]

New Hampshire: The exclusive use of the English language in all schools in the instruction of children in reading, writing, spelling, arithmetic, grammar, geography, physiology, history, civil government, music and drawing, and the compulsory teaching of English to non-English speaking persons between the ages of sixteen and twenty-one years in evening or special day schools is required. No person or corporation shall employ an individual between sixteen and twenty-one residing in a district where there is an adequate school, unless such person is in school or has been excused for a reason satisfactory to the commissioner of education.[8]

Nevada: Only a citizen of the United States or a person who has declared his intention of becoming one shall be employed in the construction of public works or in any office or department of the state. Exception is made in the case of convicts, and exchange instructors in the University, from North and South American countries.[9]

[4] *Laws of Nebraska* (1919), ch. 234, p. 991.
[5] *Ibid.*, ch. 171, p. 383.
[6] *Ibid.*, ch. 250, p. 120.
[7] *Ibid.*, ch. 140, p. 606.
[8] State Board of Education, *Laws of New Hampshire* (1921), sec. 10, p. 24; sec. 6, p. 30; sec. 40, p. 39.
[9] *Laws of Nevada* (1919), ch. 168, p. 296.

A hunting license shall not be issued to any person not a citizen of the United States.[10]

New Mexico: The possession of a shot-gun or rifle, or the hunting of wild birds, game, or fish, by unnaturalized, foreign-born residents is prohibited.[11]

Oregon: It is unlawful to display or circulate or offer for sale any newspaper or periodical except in English or unless a literal translation shall be conspicuously displayed.[12]

Utah: Every alien between the ages of sixteen and forty-five who cannot speak, read and write English with the ability required for the completion of the fifth grade shall attend evening school for at least four hours a week during the time there is such a school within two and one-half miles of his residence.[13]

Washington: No person not a citizen or one who has not filed his intention of becoming a citizen shall be permitted to teach in any common school or high school.[14]

The vast majority of Russians are but little affected by such legislation, but that they do feel that there is discrimination is shown in conversation with them and in items in their press. For example, the *Russkoye Slovo* for April 13, 1920, printed the following front page article which actually mentions nearly every one of the laws cited above.

[10] *Ibid.,* ch. 169, p. 297.
[11] Letter from the attorney general of New Mexico to the author cites State of New Mexico, *Session Laws 1921,* ch. 113.
[12] *General Laws of Oregon 1920,* ch. 17.
[13] *Laws of Utah 1919,* ch. 93.
[14] *Laws of Washington,* ch. 38, p. 82.

LIMITATION OF LAWS AGAINST FOREIGNERS IN THE DIFFERENT STATES OF AMERICA

Americans cannot understand why foreigners who have lived here for a certain time are in a hurry to return to their home country at the other side of the ocean.

*   *   *   *   *   *   *   *

The foreigners do not want to remain inferior workers, or waiters in restaurants, when with their money they can lead a much better and more independent life at home.

Many among them expect to become farmers, many will go into commerce and industry and will also exploit their own people—America has taught them a great deal.

But big American industry is worried by this migration *en masse,* it has become interested in the inner life of the immigrant and has discovered a number of laws against foreigners in the different states of America; here are some of them:

In the state of Nebraska, the foreigners have no right to have meetings except for religious purposes.

In the state of Oregon, foreigners have no right to read newspapers and magazines which are not printed in English. The same law is proposed in the states of Maryland, Kentucky and New York.

In the state of Pennsylvania, the foreigners have no right to keep dogs in their houses.

In the states of Rhode Island, South Dakota, Massachusetts and New York, the foreigners are subject to obligatory education until 21 years of age. The citizens are free from this obligation much earlier.

In Utah, the law about obligatory education applies to foreigners up to 45 years of age.

In New Hampshire, the law prohibits the employment of people between 16 and 21 years of age if they do not know the English language.

In the states of Michigan, New Hampshire, Tennessee and Washington, the foreigners have no right to teach. The same law is pending in the state of Massachusetts.

In the states of New York and Illinois, the widows of foreigners have no right to the pensions allowed by the law to American citizens.

In the state of Wyoming, a foreigner cannot act as guide in the mountains.

In the states of New York, New Jersey, Connecticut, Washington, Nebraska, Kansas, Maryland, Oregon and New Hampshire, in case of accident, a foreigner does not receive the compensations which are due to the American citizen in a similar case. This law exists, notwithstanding the fact that among foreigners there are a great many more accidents than among Americans.

In the states of Pennsylvania, Illinois, New Jersey, California, Arizona, Rhode Island, Idaho, New Mexico, Wyoming, foreigners cannot be employed for public works. In Arizona, if a foreigner tries to evade this law, he is fined $1,000, or imprisoned for six months, or both.

In the states of Massachusetts and Oregon, the same law is before the legislature. In the states of Massachusetts, New York, Washington, Illinois, Utah and Louisiana, a foreigner is accepted for employment on public works only if there is no American to be found in his place.

In the state of Idaho, the foreigner is accepted for work in a factory only if he has his first citizenship papers.

In the state of Georgia, the foreigners have no right to be peddlers. In Delaware, foreigners pay $300 a year for the right to be peddlers. In Virginia, foreigners have no right to be junk dealers. In Florida, Virginia, Texas, Washington and Ohio, foreigners cannot sell fish and oysters.

In the state of Maryland, it is proposed not to allow the foreigners to carry on commerce at all.

In the states of Illinois, California, Minnesota, Idaho, Texas, Missouri, Nebraska, Indiana, Montana, Arizona, Oklahoma, Kentucky, Iowa and Mississippi, foreigners have no right to own property, or the ownership is limited between five and twenty years. In many places, foreigners are allowed to own not more than 320 acres, or are without the right of succession.

In the state of Michigan, foreigners cannot be barbers.

In the state of Louisiana, foreigners cannot do any public printing work.

Besides these, there are many offending customs in the American attitude toward the foreigners. From all this it is plain that the relationship to the foreigners is not very warm. Foreigners having to bear all this cannot write home very enthusiastic letters about America, and, of course, they want to leave, the sooner the better.

If the work of the foreigner is appreciated, if he is needed in the mines, in the construction of subways, and for the work in the factories and farms, one must give him human rights, and one must not offend him at every step.

Although these laws are very inaccurately described and although the intent and effects of some of them seem to be exaggerated, the majority of the complaints do have some basis in the statutes. Many of the laws seem to be efforts to gain credit for "Americanization" legislation rather than to be constructive attempts to help the foreigner adapt himself to American life. Some are a part of the aftermath of war and are likely to be repealed. Many able American workers among the foreign-born decry much of this legislation. The Associate Director of the Bureau of Foreign Language Information Service of the American Red Cross has protested against the laws hampering our foreign language press.[15] One provision of "The Trading With the Enemy Act" of October 6, 1917, especially annoying to Russian publishers, has been the section which compels all foreign-language papers either to have a permit from the Post Office Department or else to file an advance copy of all matter which has to do with the war, with the government of the country, with any countries involved in the war, or with politics in general, at the local post office where it is censored. This law is still in force in 1922 despite the fact that we have long been out of a war emergency. The additional expense involved for the Russian newspapers is considerable.

Probably the income tax law has caused the Russians more difficulty than any other. As passed in 1913, it provided for the exemption of people whose income was $3,000 (if single) and $4,000 (if married), but the Treasury Department ruled that the exemption "cannot be allowed on a deduction in computing the tax of a non-resident alien." [16]

[15] *Cf.* New York *Times* Feb. 13, 1921, sec. 7, p. 4.
[16] *Treasury Decisions*, vol. 28, no. 1, p. 26.

Any alien, however, who would sign and swear to the following declaration would be considered a resident: "It is my intention to establish and maintain a residence in the United States." [17] The difficulty with this provision was that the law and the blanks were printed only in English. The Russian had no means of knowing that such an exemption existed, nor was he willing to sign his name to a blank which he could not read. Bitter experience with various kinds of exploiters had taught some and warned others that a signature to an English statement was dangerous. Furthermore, the Russians were afraid that if they signed this paper they would have to become American citizens and could not go back to Russia. Many of them had wives in the old country, nearly all had parents or brothers and sisters there and they did not care to lose the opportunity of seeing them again at the close of the war. Besides all this, the Government was at first rather lax about collections and many Russians received their wages without deduction or difficulty of any kind.

After the United States had declared war, the Government suddenly began to enforce the provisions of the act and to collect the back taxes which had been due. For those who had money in the bank, this merely meant a loss of savings and consequent misunderstanding, but where there were no savings the collector could garnishee wages. Many

[17] *Ibid.*, vol. 29, no. 13, p. 24.

Russians suddenly found that wages were withheld, without understanding why.

Matters were thus troublesome enough for the Russian in 1917, but in 1918 the Government decided to hold the employer responsible for withholding the wages of the non-resident alien to satisfy the income tax requirement. The employers had no staff ready for this task nor did they feel it was their duty to explain the provisions of the law to their employees. The Foreign Language Governmental Information Bureau of our Federal Government says that it "has complete records of thousands of aliens who were overtaxed." Of one hundred employers the Bureau investigated, only fifteen took the trouble to explain the provision to their employees in their own language. For example, one steel company employed about 10,000 Russians, who were entitled to tax exemptions if they filled out the sworn statement, but the company found it easier to continue deducting the amount from wages.[18] They had not the office force to handle these blanks and the inquiries which would result.

The hardships caused by its earlier order no doubt influenced the Treasury Department soon after the armistice to rule that any alien who would sign the following statement should be considered a resident: "I am living in the United States and have no defi-

[18] From an unpublished investigation of the Foreign Language Governmental Information Bureau transmitted to the author.

nite intention as to when (if at all) I will make any other country my home." [19] Furthermore, employers were instructed that "an alien who has been in the United States for one year and worked steadily for three months for the same employer, is to be classed as a resident, if he has no fixed purpose to leave the United States." [20] He could thus be so classed even without signing the proper form. This gave the employer an opportunity to withhold the tax or not, largely at his discretion. Furthermore, the Russian did not understand the income tax law or the various decisions affecting his payments. The statute and its interpretations changed very frequently.

In February, 1919, for example, it was further altered so that the amount employers were to deduct from non-resident aliens was increased to 8 per cent to conform to the law of 1918.[21] This created still further confusion. Mr. Polonsky of the Foreign Language Governmental Information Bureau states that "in some cases 8 per cent was deducted from non-resident aliens, in others, 12 per cent, in some others only 2 per cent." One letter out of hundreds to this bureau [22] from Russians will show the perplexity of even the educated ones:

[19] Treasury Department, Internal Revenue Income Tax Form 1078, Official Bulletin, vol. 3, no. 546, p. 9.
[20] Instruction Sheet Issued by Local Income Tax Offices to Employees of Alien Individuals.
[21] *United States Statutes at Large, 65th Congress,* vol. 40, part 1, sec. 221, p. 1072.
[22] Foreign Language Governmental Information Service Bureau.

Natrona, Pa., April 5, 1919.

I beg the Russian Bureau to help me. The Russian immigrants are not able to pay the war taxes. Some time ago I read in the papers that only those who earned more than $1000 a year have to pay the tax and only on what they earned over $1000, and I have paid $12.07. But now in the factory they withhold more, and tell me that I myself have to pay $145 for last year, and if I have to pay for this year also, I will have to pay more than $300. And so I have to work, but do not get money to live on. And please explain why they force us to take out American papers. Those who do not want to take the papers are put out of work. And if I take the papers will I be able to go back to Russia? And why did they put the Russian people in such helpless position? They do not allow us to return to Russia, and here it is now impossible to live.

And I beg the Russian Bureau to answer my prayer, and tell me what is going to become of the Russian immigrants.

The attitude of some of the U. S. Internal Revenue officers is illustrated by the fact that the president of the Russian Society of Engineers in Chicago was refused an exemption blank by subordinates in the office until he forced the matter to the Assistant Collector himself. He says, "The other Russians do not know where to get their rights and have to take out first papers, or pay enormous taxes." [22a] A government agent reports that in a large Ohio city "the Assistant Internal Revenue Officer told me that he believed every Russian was a trouble maker; that since these Russians do not want to take out their

[22a] From an unpublished letter of which the author has a copy.

first papers they should not be entitled to exemptions; that, furthermore, he did not consider it his business to instruct employees how to proceed with the various forms. From further talk with this officer, I understand that no Russian will ever get justice if he applies to this office." He says in regard to those in Pittsburgh, "These Russians decided that it is best to suffer injustice from the American Government than to ask or insist on their rights. Their previous experience in matters of this sort has taught them a good and costly lesson. Their complaints are usually unheeded, and call forth new repressions." [23]

From all this the reader can readily understand why the Russian is not favorably impressed with the laws of America as he knows them. There are laws existing for his benefit, but the Russian is largely unconscious of that fact. In the case of protective measures such as accident insurance, they mean little until he has been injured or a friend hurt, when the award seems small. In the matter of safety appliances and other welfare legislation, the Russian is either likely to know nothing about them, or else to feel that they are merely a part of his inherent right. Like most men he remembers annoying laws more than those which merely protect common rights. Thus the legislative aspects of America in the aggregate probably seem unfavorable and their net result is to make for hostility rather than friendliness toward our Government.

[23] From an unpublished letter of which the author has a copy.

Agencies of Law and Order: The Police

There are three agencies of law and order with which Russians come into very close contact: the police, the courts, and the agents of the Federal Government. The policeman is an ever present fixture of neighborhood street life, always imminent. Although he does not trouble the Russian much in ordinary times, he is to be feared. Those who have been drunk or loitering on park benches may have found to their sorrow that he could arrest them. If a housing inspector protests against fire escape incumbrances or unsanitary housing conditions, it is often a policeman who makes that protest effective. But on no particular occasion does he help the Russians with their own problems. His other duties are sufficiently numerous without exercising himself over the needs of the foreigner unless there is violation of the law. All this naturally makes the Russian more fearful of the policeman than friendly towards him even in ordinary times. During a strike period the policemen, special deputies paid by the companies, and the mounted police, all are grouped together in the mind of the foreigner as representatives of the Government.

The writer was a witness of conditions in the Lawrence, Massachusetts, Textile Strike in 1919, when hundreds of Russians were affected. With a clergyman of New York he was forcibly ordered back off the public sidewalk simply because he dared walk by a mill; he saw the police ride upon the sidewalk following strikers peaceably walking along. Although there was a state law permitting peaceful picketing, he heard a police officer, who arrested Russians on strike, swear in court that he knew of no such law.   He saw the Russians come into the union meetings with heads bandaged, claiming to have been arrested and beaten by the police.   It was the same in the U. S. Steel Strike, the Russians recounted scores of instances of alleged mistreatment.   To cite but a few: Two Russians claimed that they attempted to go to another town in Pennsylvania during the strike, but as they jumped off the train they were arrested by two deputies with drawn revolvers, and forced to pay a fine for vagrancy besides being banished from the town. Another Russian said the police came right into his house and arrested him without a warrant, after his foreman had begged him to return to work and he had refused.   The priest in Braddock told the writer that in a strike it seemed as if every time two Russians were together on the street speaking Russian they were arrested.   According to the testimony presented in the two volumes of the Inter-Church Steel Strike Report,[24] these incidents are not exceptional, but even if false or one-sided they do serve to show the kind of incidents the Russian has heard recounted.

[24] The Inter-Church World Movement, *Report on the Steel Strike of 1919, op. cit.,* pp. 238-242.   The Inter-Church World

Perhaps harsh treatment is to be expected during a strike, but the unfortunate social result is that rightly or wrongly it prejudices the mind of the Russian against our Government. The Inter-Church Commission concluded that as a result of the steel strike, "great numbers of workers came to believe that local mayors, magistrates, and police officials try to break strikes—that the local and national government not only was not their government but was government in behalf of interests opposing theirs." [25]

Courts

Not only does the Russian dislike our police but he is not much more favorably impressed with our courts. As far as his experience is concerned, this is not strange. Nothing has been written in recent times which points out so many injustices in our present legal machinery as the bulletin of the Carnegie Foundation *Justice and the Poor,* "a study of the present denial of justice to the poor."   In the introduction, after recognizing the failure of our legal machinery to keep pace with legislation, it pleads for the equality of all men before the law and says: "For no group in the citizenship of the country is this more needed than in the case of the great mass of citizens of foreign birth, ignorant of

Movement, *Public Opinion and the Steel Strike* (N. Y., 1921), pp. 174-220.
[25] *Report on the Steel Strike, op. cit.,* pp. 238 and 242.

the language, and helpless to secure their rights unless met by an administration of the machinery of justice that shall be simple, sympathetic, and patient. To such the apparent denial of justice forms the path to disloyalty and bitterness." [26] The author of this study says: "You can work as hard as you like to teach the foreign-born resident to love American institutions, but if he doesn't get fair treatment when he comes in contact with those institutions, he will think they do not deserve his respect." [27] Yet, as the report shows, there are three things at least which prevent the foreigner from getting justice: judicial delays, court costs and fees, and the expense of counsel. The New York State Commission of Immigration found

serious abuses in the interpreter systems, on which the alien's hope of justice depends; it found no instruction in our laws which would enable a well-meaning alien to remain law-abiding in the maze of our complex ordinances, department regulations, and state laws. It found few aliens able to appeal their cases, so their sentences were heavy and their situation was hopeless because of their financial inability to obtain a full review of their case. [28]

A Russian priest in Boston asserted that most of the Russian interpreters in court were dishonest, usually charged the Russian five to ten dollars for their services, and were even open to bribery. He felt that the Russian did not get justice in our courts.

[26] Smith, R. E., *Justice and the Poor* (N. Y., 1919), p. xiv.
[27] Davis, *Immigration and Americanization, op. cit.,* p. 725.
[28] *Reports of U. S. Immigration Commission 1910,* vol. 41, p. 265.

Whether or not this judgment is too severe, it reflects to some extent the viewpoint of his class, and that it has some basis in fact is shown by the investigation of Mr. Smith for the Carnegie Foundation, already referred to.

Federal Agents

It was natural that during the war the contacts of the Russian with agents of the Federal Government should be more numerous. There were liberty loans to be raised, there were disloyal elements to be dealt with, and there was an army to be conscripted. Our nation was at war and in the endeavor to win, it was almost unavoidable that little time and energy should have been devoted to observing scrupulously the rights of foreign-born residents. Since the investigations of this study were made immediately following the war, the writer naturally met a great many complaints as to war time conditions and methods. These may or may not have been just, but are worth recording briefly because they help us to understand the mind of the Russian. Some Russians seemed embittered by "the forceful methods local officials followed in compelling us to buy Liberty Bonds." "If we made any excuse for not buying we were called 'traitors,' 'cowards' and other worse words." What caused more ill feeling was the placing of Russians in the first class when they were entitled to the fifth, according to a priest in Boston. One in Cleveland said, "The Russian workers were told to sign a paper, not knowing what it was they signed and afterwards were sent to war." In Detroit the testimony was along the same line, "Some Russians who had wives and children were conscripted as soldiers because they could not speak English and no interpreter was provided. They were shamelessly treated." One Russian who was a conscientious objector said that he spent seventeen months in the Fort Leavenworth penitentiary where there were eighty-seven other Russians confined for the same reason. The Baptist pastor told the writer that this man was a very faithful church worker. The head of the Russian Consultation Bureau in Detroit who had before been in the Consulate in Chicago stated that during the war if a Russian had a wife in the home country, he had no way to prove it and so was compelled to serve in the army. Mr. Anderson, formerly head of the Y.M.C.A. work for Russians in the United States, says:

With the selective draft has come additional misunderstanding. Not knowing the language, the Russian has had difficulty in properly filling out his registration card, and in many cases he has been called for service where he should have been exempted or else put in a deferred classification. I have had my attention called to literally thousands of such supposedly unjust cases resulting from misunderstandings. The other day a Russian discharged soldier, who has a family in Russia, told me that he filled out his questionnaire and asked for exemption on the ground that he was not an

American citizen and was married. The police officer to whom he gave the questionnaire tore it up and told him he must go into the Army whether he wanted to or not; yet according to our laws this man should have been exempted. In some cases he has gone into the Army as a volunteer with a burning desire to serve his country, and in the training camp, because of his lack of knowledge of the English language, he has been assigned to the labor battalion, there to spend his days in drudgery. In the camp he has been singled out by the thoughtless American soldier and officer and has been insulted, humiliated and held up to ridicule. Such treatment has not inspired in him a love for America or Americans.[29]

Whether or not the procedure of a particular draft board seemed absolutely fair to the Russian depended, no doubt, on local conditions. At any rate, in some places the Russians had no criticism to make of its action.

The methods adopted in making the extensive raids against Communists and other "reds" were almost universally condemned by the Russians and seemed to be the cause of the greatest complaint. Between November 1, 1919, and April 26, 1920, warrants were issued by the Department of Labor for the arrest of 6,500 aliens. Approximately 3,000 of these were apprehended, although many others were temporarily arrested and then set free.[30]

[29] An unpublished statement transmitted to the author.
[30] Panunzio, C. M., *The Deportation Cases of 1919-1920* (N. Y. 1921), p. 16.

Most of the aliens involved were Russians.[31] Mr. C. M. Panunzio was given access to all the original records at Washington by the Department of Labor. He also interviewed the men who were arrested. In a careful and scientific study of 200 cases taken at random, 148, or 74 per cent were Russians.[32] Of those who were actually deported almost all were Russians.[33] The arrests were made very largely in two raids, one on the night of November 7, 1919, against the Union of Russian Workers, the other on January 2, 1920, against the Communist Party of America. Those who were attending schools, clubs, workingmen's associations, labor unions and political parties were taken into custody, even church settlements were not always immune. Often all the persons on the premises were arrested indiscriminately regardless of whether or not their names and history were known, and regardless of the lack of evidence against them. Property was destroyed, and printed matter seized and held without warrant.[34] Here again it must be remembered that although nearly a year had elapsed since the armistice, our country was still technically at war. The social mind had been sorely disturbed by publicity

[31] Letter from the Assistant Secretary of Labor, Mr. Post, to the author.

[32] Panunzio, *op. cit.,* p. 17.

[33] Department of Labor, *Annual Reports for 1920,* "Report of the Commissioner General of Immigration," pp. 312-315.

[34] *Cf.* Panunzio, *op. cit.,* pp. 24-34 and *Report of the U. S. Attorney General 1920, op. cit.,* pp. 174-177 and *Report upon the Illegal Practices of the U. S. Department of Justice* (Washington, 1920), pp. 4-5, 11-43.

concerning alleged German and Bolshevik plots. There were radical and dangerous aliens stirring up dissension, and in securing their arrest mistakes were inevitable. Apparently, however, there were inexcusable things done and many Russians suffered grievous wrongs which rankle in their minds to-day.

A report entitled *Illegal Practices of the United States Department of Justice* discussing the methods used in these raids was issued in May, 1920, by twelve eminent lawyers headed by Dean Pound of the Harvard Law School. It says:

Under the guise of a campaign for the suppression of radical activities, the office of the Attorney General, acting by its local agents throughout the country, and giving express instructions from Washington, has committed continual illegal acts. Wholesale arrests both of aliens and of citizens have been made without warrant or any process of law; men and women have been jailed and held *incommunicado* without access of friends or counsel; homes have been entered without search-warrant and property seized and removed; other property has been wantonly destroyed; workingmen and workingwomen suspected of radical views have been shamefully abused and maltreated.[35]

Because he believed the methods used were illegal Francis Fisher Kane resigned as United States District Attorney, while Judge Thompson of Pittsburgh, according to the press,[36] made the following

[35] *Report Upon the Illegal Practices of the United States Department of Justice, op. cit.,* p. 3.

[36] A prominent lawyer has informed the author that the statement was substantially correct.

comment on the case of a Russian brought to trial before him: "This case makes my blood boil. The methods of the Department of Justice have created more anarchy than all the radical parties put together, and conditions in this district are worse than they were in Russia. I did not suppose this kind of thing could happen in a country where we had a constitution." In his study Panunzio corroborated the conclusions found in the report signed by Dean Pound. He states that not even an administrative hearing was given in some cases until weeks after the Russians were imprisoned. In the hearings the immigrant inspector acted as prosecutor, judge, and jury at the same time. "In some instances the very man who originally had caused the arrest of the alien acted as interpreter at the hearing." [37] In 1922 Senator Walsh, a Democrat, a member of the Subcommittee on the Judiciary of the United States Senate, brought in a report substantiating these charges against the Department of Justice under a Democratic administration. Charles E. Hughes, now Secretary of State, has declared that the methods used, "savor of the worst practices of tyranny." [38]

The methods used in arresting and deporting can be better understood by a few concrete examples.

[37] Panunzio, *op. cit.,* p. 94.
[38] Report of Subcommittee of the Judiciary, *Charges of Illegal Practices of the Department of Justice,* 67th Congress, 2nd Session, Senate Committee Print (Washington, 1922), p. 37.

Theodore Concevich, head of the Church of All Nations in New York City, says:

> Joseph Polulech is a young Russian, twenty-five years old. He was in America eight years. He was a member of the church and I was his pastor. He is a bright young man, eager to learn. He was attending a night school run by the Communist Party. He was studying English and algebra. He was not a Communist, but he was made an officer in the school because of his faithfulness and intelligence. On the night that the school was raided by the Lusk Committee, everybody present was arrested, Joseph Polulech among them. I and others protested to the Lusk Committee and gave our guarantee that young Polulech was not a Communist. We received no reply to our protest. Joseph Polulech is now among two hundred and forty-nine aliens who are locked up in cars being pushed over the Finnish frontier.

Mr. Concevich added: "Russians are now afraid to attend public meetings and classes for fear of having the police raid their meeting places and 'beat them up.' " [39]

Dean Pound and the other lawyers, in the report already cited, secured and published a number of affidavits, which they evidently considered authentic, testifying to the brutal methods of the government agents. To cite one instance: Mitchel Layrowsky, a teacher of mathematics, swore to the following:

> I am fifty years old. I am married and have two children.

[39] Personal statement to the author.

I was principal of the Iglitsky High School for fifteen years in Odessa, Russia. I declared my intention to become a citizen of the United States. On Nov. 7, 1919, I conducted a class at 137 East 15th St., New York. At about eight o'clock in the evening, while I was teaching algebra and Russian, an agent of the Department of Justice opened the door of the school and walked in with a revolver in his hands and ordered everybody in the school to step aside. Then he ordered me to step toward him. I wore eyeglasses and the agent of the Department of Justice ordered me to take them off. Then he struck me on the head and simultaneously two others struck me and beat me brutally. After I was without strength to stand up, I was thrown downstairs; and while I rolled down, other men beat me with pieces of wood, which I later found were obtained by breaking the banisters. I sustained a fracture of the head, left shoulder, and right side. Then I was ordered to wash myself and was taken to 13 Park Row, where I was examined and released about midnight. [40]

That this was not an isolated instance can be seen by referring to other exhibits from the authorities already quoted. For example, in Mr. Panunzio's study Necita Zafronia testified, "I have lived long enough in Russia, under the Czar. I have seen brutality committed there, but I have never seen the brutality that was committed on the Russian people here." [41] On the other hand, large numbers were arrested without such extreme treatment

[40] *Report on the Illegal Practices of the U. S. Department of Justice, op. cit.,* p. 18.
[41] *The Deportation Cases of 1919-1920, op. cit.,* p. 77.

though naturally experiencing great inconvenience, loss of wages, and even the loss of positions.

The way Russians themselves expressed their feelings to the author is shown in the following statements given by Russians imprisoned on Ellis Island. How true all the statements are is open to question, but the subsequent release of many indicates at least that the Government did not always substantiate its charges. Steve —— was twenty-five years old and had been in America seven years. For the last five he had been working in the Newark Tube Metal Works. He was arrested along with everyone else in a restaurant. He claimed he was not a Communist, although he had been a socialist, and thought his detention was due to his having contributed money to aid imprisoned Russians. He said:

In Russia I was frequently maltreated and had a difficult life as a peasant, but I never did anything against the government. In the United States I am not opposed to your form of government and have never favored the use of force. I believe all the Russians here are treated unjustly, their jobs are taken away, they are arrested; at the same time they are denied passports to return to Russia. The Czar's régime, bad as it was, never treated its subjects as the Russians are being treated at the present time in America.

Joe —— was a member in good standing of the International Union of Mine and Smelter Workers of America, for the author saw his union card. He had been arrested in his home at midnight. He claimed that he was not even a socialist, but was enrolled in an arithmetic class, meeting in a Russian Club. During the month that he had been held at Ellis Island he did not know what had become of his wife and five children, as they had no money. He felt that in this matter the American Government had treated him and his family most unjustly.

Another Russian had been employed as a fireman in the American Brass Company. He was detained for over two months only to be released because it was found that instead of belonging to a Communist society, he was a member of an educational group. Out of 200 cases selected at random, Mr. Panunzio found that 47 were not members of a proscribed society and that only 56 clearly did so belong. In justice to the Government, the tangible results of these raids in freeing America from undesirable aliens should be noted. At least 810 were ordered deported by the Secretary of Labor, and between July 1, 1919, and June 30, 1920, 314 actually were sent to Europe.[42] The author heard radical Russians admit that from the standpoint of a "capitalistic" government some of the arrests were justified. It is probably true that this action also made the rank and file of Russians think twice before becoming members of an organization. They were less

[42] Department of Labor, *Annual Reports for 1920, op. cit.,* pp. 312-315.

likely to join without knowing what its constitution and principles were.

Nevertheless, the methods employed and the publicity given have caused widespread injustice and harsh feeling where it was unnecessary. In Duquesne, Pennsylvania, a representative of a government bureau lecturing on "Abraham Lincoln and American Democracy" to Russians was arrested and imprisoned as a Bolshevik because he lectured in Russian. It took the Government thirty-six hours to free its own agent. He says: "After they found out who I was and set me free, I asked the mayor of the city whether he would allow me to deliver my lecture now. He said that he would not. I am convinced that no propaganda could be more effective in spreading animosity towards the American Government." [43] In Boston, a Greek Orthodox priest told the author that things reached such a pass in his neighborhood that a crowd of Americans gathered and threw stones and tin cans at any one who entered the church. Once he even had to get a policeman to conduct him from his home to the religious service.

It can hardly be denied that the results of the raids have been to increase the misunderstanding between the Russian and our Government. On this point, Mr. Panunzio concludes: "As a consequence of all this (the raids, arrests and imprisonments), a volume of prejudice and suspicion has been pro-

[43] Taken from a letter from the government representative.

duced among immigrant groups which it will require
perhaps years to allay." [44]   On the whole, the relationship between federal agents and the Russian is
one more of the circumstantial factors which neither
makes him see the best in America nor stimulates
him to love our institutions.

The Effect of the Russian Revolution

The Russian revolution has also had a decided
effect on the Russian's attitude toward our Government.   Before that event, in spite of some unsatis-
factory conditions here, most Russians felt that, on
the whole, their circumstances would be much worse
in Tsarist Russia.   After the revolution the aspect of
affairs changed; the Russian did not know, but he
believed that there was a vast improvement in Russia.   He was a warm believer in the revolution and
no matter who was controlling the government, at
least it proclaimed itself a régime of the workers.
The event gave the Russian here opportunity to give
vent to his self-assertive or egoistic tendencies which,
as we have already seen, were largely repressed in
his home and occupational life.   If in America he
was considered an inferior, at least his own country
and his own people had been the first to lead the
world in a workers' commonwealth.   "I would be
a free man and a member of the only real workers'
government in the world, if I could only reach

[44] *The Deportation Cases of 1919-1920, op. cit.,* p. 96.

Russia," one said to the author. Russian priests, the Russian consul, editors of the Russian papers, all testified that the majority of the Russians here were sympathetic to the Bolsheviks and in favor of the Soviets. If in 1922 some were growing a little less cordial toward the Bolsheviks, they remained just as warm supporters of the Soviets as ever.[45]

But the United States opposed the Bolsheviks. American soldiers were sent to Siberia and Archangel. The Government until 1920 refused to permit Russians to return to their homeland. At the same time, speeches made by Senators Johnson, France, and others assailing our Russian policy were widely circulated by the Russian papers. All these facts powerfully stimulated the feeling against the American Government. It was the opinion of a priest in Boston who was interviewed that fifty per cent of the men who were not Bolsheviks at first, sympathized with them later because of the action of the United States Government. The one in Buffalo who was himself an American citizen said that almost none of the Russians knew the good side of America. "They ask, why does the Government tax us, why arrest us, why not permit us to go home?" According to a report sent by a Russian-speaking American investigator in California in 1920, "With few exceptions, the Russians want to go home. Recently all the Molokans, of Tacoma, San

---

[45] Statement of Omeltchenko, Vilchur, Polonsky and many other Russians.

Francisco, Los Angeles and along the coast, number-
ing several thousand, requested the Government to
deport them. They claimed that they had been
'cheated' by the Americans in their talk about the
'freedom of America.' " The head of the Russian
Consultation Bureau in Detroit and formerly in the
Russian Consulate in Chicago expressed the reason
thus: "The Russians do not understand the United
States and the United States does not understand
them. Before the war, many took out citizenship
papers but not now after the Bolshevik revolution."
The revolution profoundly affected the Russian's
attitude toward our Government and it no less profoundly affected the attitude of our Government and
people toward the Russian. The result was that
each was becoming increasingly suspicious towards
the other. Some Russians became dangerous radicals favoring a world revolution. The Government
made wholesale arrests, and mutual distrust was the
inevitable result. It is but another illustration of
what sociologists have long recognized to be true,
that unlike individuals reacting toward each other
in unlike ways make for conflict.

Conclusion

The foregoing evidence makes it clear that in an
unfortunately large number of cases, legislation,
to the Russian mind, has been discriminatory, con-
fiscatory, or otherwise unjust. The agencies of law
and order also appear to him to have been organized

to serve Americans, not Russians. As a foreign-born worker he has been looked down on in America; in Russia his country has achieved a new form of government—of the workers, for the workers, and by the workers—so he thinks. The revolution in his homeland has strengthened his self-esteem and given outlet to his desire for recognition. This stimulates his discontent with America where he realizes that he is at the bottom of the social scale. The raids and wide-spread arrests in 1919 and 1920 accentuated this feeling and created a sense of injustice in the mind of the Russian. All these facts have undoubtedly made for misunderstanding and mutual distrust between the Russian and our Government. From our American standpoint we can dismiss these various factors with easy explanations; or we can with deeper insight understand that they are due to war psychology, mutual unlikeness, and absorption in our own affairs. But to the incoming alien, America has beckoned as the Utopia of his own individual dreams. What wonder if the disillusionment has been bitter!

CHAPTER VII

America's Contribution to the Russian

A CAREFUL consideration of the data already presented should have given a reasonably clear picture of the relationship of the average Russian worker to the rest of our American society. Because the facts have shown so much unlikeness and misunderstanding between ourselves and the Russian aliens it is well to review briefly the real contribution which America offers.

In the first place until very recently she has generously thrown wide her doors to all sorts and conditions of Russians except the mere handful of those defective in mind or body. The illiterate masses have not in the past been discriminated against, and political and religious refugees have found no obstacles to entrance, nor have they been deported even in the face of demands from the Tsar's Government.

All these Russians have in the end secured some employment which in prosperous times has permitted many of them to save. They have had an opportunity to share in the boundless material resources of America in some measure, even though it be only a stake in the daily pay roll. Large sums have, in the aggregate, been sent by them to the homeland and considerable numbers have returned to Russia with accumulations of money which seemed fabulous to the simple peasants of their home districts. Others have risen to positions of comfort and prosperity on the farms or in the cities of the land of their adoption. To some of them has come a new sense of freedom of opportunity for individual initiative; some among them have here the chance to read in the Russian newspapers material which might have been censored or declared illegal under the Tsar. A large number of libraries, welfare, and educational institutions, moreover, are open to them, and to perhaps an increasingly large number bring a new aspect of America, a faint conception of our traditions and our ideals. One Russian who had been illiterate at the time of his entry, after eight months' study in a civic center, wrote the following: "While in Russia . . . I could not understand how people can govern themselves. Now that I have spent nearly eight months in this country, I came to the conclusion that a democratic government is more advantageous than a monarchial."[1] Another clearly recognized that this country has liberty of conscience, free press, and free speech, "Therefore, the Russian people are coming here because they haven't this in their country."

Furthermore, married Russians with children

[1] Davis, *Immigration and Americanization* (Boston, 1920), p. 662.

come to realize something of what free education means—that it is a gift of immeasurable value. The second generation read and write English, they know something of our history and ideals; they are definitely becoming assimilated. As far as their social heritage is concerned, it is almost more American than Russian. Besides these there are some few foreign-born Russians—and it is to be hoped their number is increasing—who have themselves found out the real values America has to bestow, have acquired citizenship, and have to some degree become a part of the body politic. To these America offers the opportunity to enter into a common social heritage, an amalgam of the best of all.

Isolation and Unlikeness of Foreign-born Russians

In spite of all that America gives, we have seen that the great majority of Russian immigrants are isolated and remain almost totally unlike the American people. When they first arrive, they come with a cultural heritage so totally at variance with that of the American that they form a distinct non-resembling group in our society. In language, occupation, education, and *mores,* they are unlike our average. As might be expected of two unlike groups reacting on each other, segregation and mutual non-comprehension result. In the economic world the Russian has the worst task, out of touch with his employer, in contact with a foreman or boss who is often himself foreign-born. In his home life we find him occupying unsanitary, overcrowded tenements or frame buildings in the foreign districts of our cities detached from American life. Even his marketing is conducted directly with the foreign shopkeeper of his own district.

In the matter of health the foreigner is worse off than he was before coming to this country and in his recreational activities, besides being deprived of the simple folk pastimes to which he was accustomed, he has practically no choice other than the lowest amusement resorts represented by the saloon, the pool room, the dance hall, and the moving picture theater. To a considerable extent the various religious and educational forces either do not reach him at all or, as may be the case with his radical clubs and the Russian church, still further set him apart. We have seen that the various representatives and agencies of our Government have failed to break down to any extent these barriers of unlikeness, and, as one result of the wave of intolerance which swept over the social mind during and immediately following the war, considerable injustice was done the Slav: his mind was still further antagonized and made unlike that of America. All of these forces make up the sum of the social influences which the Russian takes in and incorporates as his conception of America. Each group with whom he comes in contact, each environmental factor registers on his personality an impression.   In so far as he is in a receptive, imitative attitude some of the influences such as a fund of job phrases and "swear words," or cheap liquor and questionable amusements, become a part of his own personality.   On the other hand, his self has already been cast in the mold of all the hereditary and environmental forces by which he was influenced in Russia.   In personal relations largely isolated from the best of America, he can see in large measure only that which is hostile to, that which conflicts with the best of the old social heritage.   There is little which actually bridges the Atlantic of social differences separating the American and the Russian.   Consequently, between the two there is an almost total lack of consciousness of kind.

At the beginning of this study we declared, "If the social point of view which the foreigner brings with him, and the social forces which are to act upon him are known, the attitude which the majority of his nationality will take toward the foreign country to which it comes can be predicted."   In view of the evidence we have presented, we can safely conclude that the great majority of the Russians do not understand or love America.   As a matter of fact, they look at her through the colored glasses of their experience.   It is a sociological truism that we are imposing on the average Russian a life of such limited happiness, such restrictions on the economic and social side of life, such a thwarting of normal instinctive response, that it is impossible for sympathy, coöperation and friendship to result. Our treatment of Russians is sociologically unsanitary. The following answers represent the spirit of America to a large number of Russian workmen and priests. They are surprisingly alike:

"No heart in American life."

"Busy and business."

"Each help self."

"Rich man's land."

"Money."

"Love of self."

"There is no sympathy here."

One priest in order to illustrate his conception of America went to the door and pointing to the mountain of coal dust and cinders at the mouth of the mine nearby said, "That is the heart of America."

Some expressed the conviction that America for them at least was bad.

"If money in pocket Americans like you, if not don't care and swear at you."

"America place like heaven for rich, but like hell for foreign worker."

"As a wild animal or bird in a cage, so lives the Russian here."

"America is not free for the workers. They are beasts like horses."

"I think American if he has condition as has foreign man, became long ago as Bolshevik."

"To-day we Russians are friendless. Hatred is

preached against us everywhere. The word Russian is enough to make an enemy, and put one in danger."

"At home we have a Tsar, here we have a superintendent."

These quotations represent in a vague and incoherent way the attitude of thousands of Russians toward our country. On the other hand, the American group for its part does not comprehend the Russian. The head of the Russian consultation bureau in Detroit expressed the present relationship between the two groups when he said, "The Russians do not understand the United States, and the United States does not understand the Russians."

The workers sense this misunderstanding, as is evidenced by the following: "Even in opinion of middle class in America, the Russian workmen are the animal." "Experience has taught us that Americans should be regarded as exploiters, they look on us as 'Polacks.' " The Russian newspapers clearly reveal the same attitude, as in the following:

Russki Golos, April 20, 1920

(A Translation)

DO YOU LIKE AMERICA?

"If you don't—get out," says the landlord to his tenant. Masters of American land—they are the landlords, too. What they are used to saying to their tenants, they say to the immigrant masses. By their order, articles are written in newspapers which are read all over the country. They dictate the words that are shown in brilliant letters on the screen in moving pictures. Every day these words stand before the people's eyes, are whispered in their ears. They poison the soul of the American people with spite and stupid arrogance. These offensive words are daily thrown into the newcomer-immigrant's face. "If you don't like it— get out," says the landlord to his tenant. "If you don't like this country—get out," shout the capitalistic newspapers and moving pictures to the immigrant laborer.

"Get out of here," is told to the immigrant. These words are not only stupid, they are false. If millions of workmen who came here from Europe should leave the U. S., America's strength and wealth would vanish. In the big theaters among dancing and other entertainments you see these same words on the screen:—"If you don't like this country— get out." Many would like to get out and will do it as soon as possible. But is it true that we do not like this country? We like this country as any country. Here also the sun shines, the woods murmur and the rivers flow. This country is a good field for human labor. As everywhere else, here are people humiliated by the strong ones. As everywhere else the money bag is ruling.

It is not that we do not like America. We do not like the great amount of violence and falsehood that is in America. We do not like it that in America are stupid people. They are among those who throw in the face of the Russian and European workman, who have helped to create the wealth of America the offensive words, "Get out of here."

Russkoye Slovo, Dec. 24, 1920

(A Translation)

America is not at all interested in the soul and spiritual life of the Russian immigrant, only in his muscles. He came to this country a stranger and often leaves it again without any American knowing him at all. It is therefore very unjust to accuse him of disloyalty, ingratitude and revolt.

Need of Increasing the Likeness Between the Russian and American Mind

In view of all this, the need of creating a greater likeness between the Russian and the American mind seems entirely obvious. If we are ever to get a group consciousness, a patriotic devotion to American ideals by all, it must be accomplished by breaking down the barriers now existing. We unhesitatingly spent large sums in arresting thousands of Russians suspected of radicalism and Bolshevism in 1919 and 1920. This was merely a striking proof that America had herself failed to provide the necessary social mechanism to create mutual understanding. In this connection it is important to note that those Russians who were arrested as dangerous anarchists by our Government at that time were those who had had almost no contacts with Americans at all. With the permission of the Assistant Secretary of Labor, the writer interviewed arrested Russians in Detroit, Pittsburgh, Hartford, and Ellis Island. Each Russian was asked whether, during his stay in America, he had ever met any American who had helped him. It was suggested that perhaps there had been some teacher, some boss, some boarding-house keeper or worker who had been friendly to him. Out of nearly

150 arrested Russians there were only five who had ever received any such aid. Of these American friends, two had been workmen, two company doctors, and one a teacher. On the other hand, every one of the groups had met many who had cursed them, foremen who called them "Russian swine," bosses who were continually swearing at them. America, according to their stories, had been for the most part one constant struggle against adverse industrial conditions and exploitation. The former head of the Russian work of the Y.M.C.A. in America after speaking in the various Russian colonies says: "At practically every place I have visited, I have been hailed as one of the first Americans to come to him (the Russian) extending a friendly hand. Sometimes he has shed tears, while occasionally he has cursed America, and included me along with her." The result of this lack of intercourse is that thousands of Russians who have become skilled in our industrial processes return to Europe just at the time when, having learned their trades, they are at the point of maximum efficiency. If we could bring about a greater likemindedness between the Russian and the American it would increase coöperation in every factory, mine, and community where the Slav is employed. It also goes without saying that if the foreign-born Russian could be made to understand the best of America, it would enormously aid in fitting the second generation to meet the opportunities and duties of citizenship.

Theodore Roosevelt clearly realized this when he said in an address on Americanism in 1915,[2] "We cannot afford to continue to use hundreds of thousands of immigrants merely as industrial assets while they remain social outcasts and menaces."

We owe these foreigners a moral obligation. As Dr. Giddings says,[3] "Society is morally responsible for the costs of its existence." The Slavic workers are essential parts of our economic mechanism. A prominent manufacturer in Lawrence, Massachusetts, admitted to the writer that the textile mills would never be able to keep running were it not for the foreign labor. "Americans would refuse to do the dirty work," was his comment. The U. S. Immigration Commission in 1909 [4] found that four fifths of the operatives of thirty-eight great industries were either foreign-born or the sons of foreigners. The proportion would probably be still higher in 1922, for it has been since 1909 that the heaviest immigration has come, displacing still further American unskilled labor. But it is precisely in the essential industries such as iron and steel, coal mining, railway construction, meat packing, and sugar refining that we find the Russian worker. Ex-President Wilson has said:

The welfare, the happiness, the energy and spirit of the

[2] Address given before the Knights of Columbus, Carnegie Hall, New York, October 13, 1915, reprinted in Davis, *op. cit.,* p. 645.

[3] Giddings, *Democracy and Empire, op. cit.,* p. 86.

[4] *Abstracts of Reports of the Immigration Commission,* vol. 1, *op. cit., passim.*

men and women who do the daily work in our mines and factories, on our railroads, in our offices and ports of trade, on our farms, and on the sea, is the underlying necessity of our prosperity. There can be nothing wholesome unless their life is wholesome; there can be no contentment unless they are contented. Their physical welfare affects the soundness of the whole nation.[5]

But it is futile to pretend we have made our foreign workers happy and contented, least of all the Russians. Rabbi Wise of the Free Synagogue in New York City says: "I would have America either shut foreigners out or take them in, not leave them dangling in spirit at our doors, physically admitted to, but spiritually excluded from, the life of the Republic." [6]

Moreover, can we really be a democracy if large elements of the population are thus detached? The publication, *Americanization,* of the United States Department of Education, asks the following searching questions:

What should be said of a world-leading democracy wherein ten per cent of the adult population cannot read the laws which they are presumed to know?

What should be said of a democracy which sends an army to preach democracy wherein there was drafted out of the first 2,000,000 men a total of 200,000 men who could not read their orders or understand them when delivered?

What should be said of a democracy which expends in a year twice as much for chewing gum as for school books,

[5] Wilson, *The New Freedom* (N. Y., 1918), p. 290.
[6] From an unpublished address sent in manuscript to the author.

more for automobiles than for all primary and secondary education, and in which the average teacher's salary is less than that of the average day laborer?

What should be said of a democracy which permits men and women to work in masses where they seldom or never hear a word of English spoken? [7]

Possible Methods of Securing Like-mindedness

The chief purpose and findings of this study have now been presented, the actual situation and relationship of the Russians in our social structure has been at least partially diagnosed. Their treatment and experience seem to shut them out from and keep them unlike our normal American group. It is not intended to outline the concrete methods which must be followed to break down the isolation which is the key to the present situation. This would involve a further careful and much more exhaustive study. Certain things, however, can be urged. In the first place, the barriers to communication between the two peoples must be overthrown. Inter-stimulation, communication and response must in some way be established between them. One of the chief obstacles to this is the language barrier. To know where the aliens are is the first step. The State Department of Americanization in New York had copied from the U. S. Census record the names and addresses of all people 21 to 50 years of age who were listed as not

[7] *Americanization,* Jan. 1, 1919, p. 3.

able to read or write any language or not able to speak English:

The 381,000 names which were copied from the census schedules were distributed among the 320 superintendents of schools of New York State. In many cities and villages, local school boards appointed teachers to visit these people at their homes to invite them to attend classes for the study of English and citizenship. We estimate that about 100,000 homes were visited during the past school year. In these visits to the homes, teachers probably carried the message of the public school to about 300,000 foreign-born, as they met five or six persons on every such visit.[8]

Such a procedure must, of course, be followed by some definite contact with those whose names are secured, as seems to have been done to some extent in this case. To eradicate the differences of language, two things are essential. Adequate schools at the right hours and in the right localities for the foreigners should be provided by the community or the state. Second, the proper relationship with the immigrants must be sustained in order to induce them to attend such classes. This might be accomplished by having foreign-speaking workers attached to the schools, who would maintain friendly contacts with the foreigners and let them know what the schools offered and where they were.

Provided it were possible to enlist the coöperation of the employer, this would be the quickest and

---

[8] Letter of the Supervisor of Immigrant Education for the State of New York to the author.

easiest way to help the Russian learn English. As
W. M. Roberts, Assistant Superintendent of Schools
in Chicago, said at the National Americanization
Conference in 1919: [9] "If the employers representing the dominant industries in any industrial city
remain indifferent as to whether or not the foreign-
born men in their employ know the English language,
it requires extraordinary effort on the part of other
agencies of the community to get them started in
learning English. The experiences growing out of
the war have shown that the foreign-born men would
like to be called Americans; that they would prefer
to speak English in the shop and on the street, and
that they have not learned, largely because it was
not required of them in the factory, was not necessary at home, and they could get all the news they
wanted out of the foreign language newspapers."

If a law could be enacted which prohibited
manufacturers from employing any alien who did
not read and write English unless the manufacturer
established in his plant a class for such aliens under
the direction of the local board of education, it
might prove effective. The law should also provide
that the foreigners were to attend the class during
their working hours on company time. Such a law
would enormously stimulate the desire of the
foreigner to learn English, and it would force the
employer, utilizing the cheapest foreign labor, to
install English classes in English.

[9] Davis, *Immigration and Americanization, op. cit.,* p. 714.

The D. E. Sicher Company of New York has adopted such a plan and when asked whether classes to teach employees were worth while, one of its officers said: "On the basis of expense also, I could prove to you that it is worth while. . . . Four years ago the company organized classes in the plant for instruction in English, the New York City Board of Education providing the teacher. Fifty-five girls were enrolled in three groups, each one receiving instruction for three-quarters of an hour each morning, wages being paid during that time." The results showed a steady increase in hourly wages and a decrease in the number of supervisors needed.[10]

The Wisconsin Bridge and Iron Company of Milwaukee has for several years paid one hour's wages to every non-English-speaking employee studying English in the school room.[11] In a letter of January 6, 1922, to the author, the vice-president of this concern says that they have been very much pleased with the remarkable progress made by those who are studying and that they believe the policy has resulted in a better feeling between the foreign employees and the company.

Massachusetts has taken the lead in the coöperation between the state department of education and the manufacturers and the local communities. The state provides half the funds and the local communities the other half for classes in industry

[10] *Americanization,* June 1, 1919, p. 10 (also *cf.* MacCarthy, *Where Garments and Americans Are Made* (N. Y., 1917), pp. 1-55.
[11] *Ibid.,* Feb. 1, 1919, p. 10.

under a local director of immigrant education and a trained group of teachers equipped with text books. The industries organize a committee or plant director, recruit classes, provide the class-room facilities and provide incentives. In December, 1921, thirty-eight cities and fifty-four towns in Massachusetts took advantage of the state law and organized such classes.[12]

Next to the language barrier comes that of misunderstanding and ignorance, which is closely linked up with that of exploitation. Here also there is no single easy method by which to demolish the obstruction. One means toward this end would be the establishment by the Federal Government of information bureaus for aliens in the more important foreign centers. The bureaus should be managed by naturalized citizens under the direction of an American; at least one foreign-speaking worker for each major nationality in the city. They would be prepared among other things to tell the inquirer where to find good lawyers, doctors, banks, night schools, and welfare agencies, besides tracing out and exposing exploitation and fraud. Such a bureau could also assist in giving American news items to the foreign-language press. As a matter of fact, the Foreign Language Governmental Information Service Bureau did exactly this in a small way during the war and at the present time the work is being

[12] Letter from the Assistant State Supervisor of Americanization to the writer.

continued by the American Red Cross. The difficulty is that they are now able to maintain only one
office in New York, whereas one should be found
in every large center of the foreign-born. In spite
of this fact the bureau gives out news to 795 foreign-
language publications, covering eighteen foreign
language groups, who print an average of three-
quarters of a million words per month of this
material.[13] It has sent out 95,000 pamphlets in
Russian, Ukranian, Hungarian and Polish and
adjusts more than 2000 personal cases a month. "It
furnishes 30,000 words of foreign-language editorial
matter to 100 American papers monthly and sends
5000 words of general news concerning the alien to
400 papers." [14]

The creation of such an information bureau has
for a long time been strongly urged on the Government by competent authorities. At the time when
the United States Immigration Commission was
making a study of the entire immigration problem
a letter was sent out to the various welfare
organizations working among immigrants asking,
"What, in your opinion, can the National Government do to promote assimilation or Americanization
of immigrants?" Nearly all of those who replied
recommended some form of informational help to
the immigrant, and eight specifically mentioned some

[13] Bierstadt, E. H., "The Work of the Foreign Language Information Service," *The Legal Aid Review,* vol. 19, no. 4 (Oct., 1921),
p. 3.
[14] *Ibid.,* p. 6.

form of an information bureau.[15] More recently the Secretary of the California Immigration Commission has urged the establishment of a Federal agency to coöperate with the states. "Each state must establish a central commission with the responsibility for developing and executing a state program of Americanization, properly coördinated with the national program. Second, the National Government must establish a central agency charged with the full power of a broad national Americanization program carried on in coöperation with the state."[16] In the report of the United States Commissioner of Education for 1919 it is recommended that an "immediate national organization of all forces," public and private, under the leadership of the Federal Government, should be created. "The problem is too delicate to be left to the uncertain activities of undirected amateurs."[17] Enough concrete plans have been proposed. The need is for action. There is a real danger that since the war is over, all such plans will be abandoned. As ex-President Roosevelt said in one of his last public statements, "There must be no sagging back in the fight for Americanism merely because the war is over."[18]

If the Government should establish some form of

[15] Reports of the Immigration Commission, vol. 41, *op. cit., passim.*
[16] *Americanization* (Conference Supplement), June 1, 1919, p. 11.
[17] U. S. Bureau of Education, *Report of the Commissioner of Education* (1919), p. 46.
[18] *Americanization,* Feb. 1, 1909, p. 7.

information bureau on an adequate scale, it would to a large extent break down misunderstanding, exploitation, and unlikeness. Such agencies would also serve to help in educating Americans about Russians. Nearly all the foreign groups would be glad to see such a service carried on and the Russians would certainly be no exception. The *Russkoye-Slovo* for Nov. 17, 1919, made the following comment in this connection:

A number of organizations are helping the immigrant understand the political, social and industrial life in this country. Nothing, however, seems to be done to teach Americans to know the immigrant, his aims and desires. The average American knows little about the foreign-born. He considers every Italian a member of the "Black Hand" Society. He thinks that every Russian is a Bolshevik, every German an admirer of the Kaiser. Until the war, Americans were not interested in European life and people. For example, a popular magazine published a picture representing a Jew from Warsaw and a Caucasian mountaineer, entitling it: "Russian Types from Russia in General." An official organization asked the governor how many Russians there were in his state. The official replied, "In the city of N on X Street, there are many Russians of Jewish descent. We have no information about other Russians." It is true that during the first period of immigration from Russia, Jews and Poles predominated, therefore, Americans conclude that the population of Russia chiefly consists of them. Before Americans can attempt to Americanize the immigrant, they must study his life and culture.

That this feeling of a Russian editor has some

foundation in fact, the present study has demonstrated. In order to assimilate the foreigner we must break down prejudice on both sides, American as well as Russian. Says President W. G. Harding: [19]

The person of foreign birth is more a victim in this country than a conspirator, because agitators have been preaching the gospel of revolution to him incessantly, whereas no one so far seems to have preached to him the blessings of an orderly government and the rewards of American opportunity. America, that has invited and enlisted foreign manpower for its industries, has even neglected to teach the immigrant the American language. It is far more important to practice than to preach "Americanism."

The few remedies here proposed are merely suggestions. This study has attempted to describe conditions, not to prescribe cures. It has demonstrated the fact that the foreign-born Russians at present are isolated and out of touch with the average American life. In some way the barriers to assimilation must be broken down. A scientific solution of the problem now will save America continual social loss, and possible crisis in the future.

[19] *Foreign Born,* March, 1920, p. 19.

APPENDIX

THE SOCIAL IMPRESS OF AN AUTOCRACY [1]

A Peasant Immigration

THE Russians who have come streaming to our shores in such great numbers have not carried with them large accumulations of material wealth, nor have they been burdened with the usual tourists' conglomeration of boxes and bags. Their baggage has been of a different sort. It consisted in the social heritage of an autocracy. Unalterably opposed to the Tsar's tyranny as was the United States Government, yet she could not force these newcomers to check this peculiarly personal baggage, the social impress of an autocracy, at the door. It was brought in and carried far and wide wherever the Russian went.

From the investigation conducted by the Immigration Commission we know that 92 per cent of the Russians migrating to the United States belonged to the peasant laboring class. Over ninety-

[1] This chapter is inserted in the Appendix because it deals with conditions in Russia rather than America. It may help toward an appreciation of the Russian's state of mind as he confronts an entirely new situation. Considerable of the material appeared in a different form in the *Political Science Quarterly,* June, 1922. For further information on the Russian background consult the *United States Immigration Reports,* vol. 4, pp. 239-348.

five out of every hundred were over sixteen years of age. Their minds had been definitely molded by the social institutions of Russia, and their view of America, as we have seen, has been warped by that process.

Land Holdings

In order to understand the outlook which they bring with them, we shall consider briefly their condition in Russia. From the liberation of the serfs in the sixties until the pre-war period, the amount of land held by the individual peasant had fallen nearly one-half. A large number of peasants had lost all their land by either renting it for a long period or by going to work for wages. In 1900 the average amount held had fallen to 2.6 dessytines, or about seven acres. Since that time, owing to the rapid increase of population, there has been a still greater shortage. Land hunger became especially acute in the provinces of Kiev, Podalsk, Poltava, Kursk and Tulsk. This probably contributed to the emigration from these districts.

Agricultural Backwardness

Besides an unequal distribution of the land, Russia has been afflicted with agricultural backwardness. Wooden plows and harrows were in common use; ropes or fiber thongs were the chief material for the harness of carts or plows. Where the *mir* existed, the land was owned in common by the entire village. Each peasant received a narrow strip between two and ten yards wide, but even where there was no *mir*, the strip system of ownership prevailed. This enormously increased the difficulties of production, but individual industry and initiative were dulled still further by the fact that, under the *mir*, in order to insure fairness, the holdings were reapportioned every few years. In addition, shiftless, slow and easy-going habits met with little rebuke under the communal system. Regardless of how little or how much improvement a peasant had made on his land, he was liable to lose it at the next redistribution. Even where there was private ownership, the wasteful three-field system, whereby one-third of the land lay idle each year, still prevailed.

Conditions in Industry

It is no wonder that increasing numbers left the soil to enter industry. By 1908 there were over a million and a half factory workers in Russia. But here, too, conditions were very hard. In 1900 the average pay of an adult male worker was only about twenty roubles a month. This necessitated an extremely low standard of living. For example, two families would often share one room. The hours of work were long, seldom averaging less than twelve a day, and the men were not permitted to organize. It is true, the same speed and machine-like efficiency that one finds in an American factory were absent; the worker was able to go more slowly and get more rest, but his lot was not an enviable one.   Although organization was not permitted, secret unions with their accompaniment of radical agitators and socialistic and anarchistic literature abounded.   The workers were taught to believe that in reality they should own and control the factories and receive "all the product of their toil."

The Peasants' Attitude toward the Land

Conditions in industry, however, were not sufficiently attractive to tempt the great mass of the peasants, and besides, they loved the land and "the work in the fields as they loved no other kind of work."   They speak of the land in such endearing terms as "mother-earth," "drink-giver" and "food-giver."   But the peasant thought that he was entitled to all he produced.   Perhaps he was not getting it, but he believed that he would when once the "greedy landlords" were dispossessed.   In the peasant courts, where law is administered on the basis of custom and folk-ways, labor is recognized as "having rights superior to property and even kinship."   Sons-in-law, stepsons and adopted sons have all the inheritance rights of children born in the home, and the first-born son is debarred if he does not take part in the common work.

The Coöperative Movement

The close village life, the economic needs of the people and a lack of the means of transportation, as well as a severe climate have all tended to foster the coöperative movement in Russia. In spite of much governmental interference, there were in 1905 about 5,800 local societies in Russia. By 1912 these had increased to 18,083 locals, with a membership of 5,760,000 "householders," and at the beginning of 1919 the number of societies had increased to 80,000, with 20,000,000 householders.

The Russian peasants crave society and all live together in a village. The little wooden huts with thatched roofs usually contain but one room and a shed. The one room combines kitchen, dining, living and bedrooms, besides being used for a calf-pen, pig-sty, or horse-stall in cold weather. In summer, when the children sleep outside, the doors and windows are open, and the entire family spends the day in the fields, perhaps the one room is adequate. In winter, when all sleep in the one room and the windows and doors are tightly closed, conditions are not so satisfactory, but even then the huge oven on which part of the family sleeps must cause some change of air in the loosely built hut. The congestion is bad, but it is usually limited to one household —although this may include daughters-in-law.

Health

The diet of the peasant is largely vegetarian, since meat is expensive. His bill of fare is made up chiefly of rye bread, potatoes, milk products, and the various vegetables in season, fresh from his own fields. Nevertheless, famines recur periodically and then thousands starve, as they did in 1891 and in 1899. Disease is prevalent owing to the lack of sanitation and doctors. In America we have one physician to every 800 persons, but in European Russia, in 1912, there was only one for every 13,000 in the cities and towns, and one for every 21,900 in the country.

The Family

The Russian peasant usually has a large family, as is evidenced by the rapid increase of the population as a whole, in spite of the high death rate. A woman works at least as hard, if not harder, than her husband. She usually milks the cow, feeds the poultry and live stock, cooks, washes, cares for the children, and in summer toils in the fields with the men. The children early begin to work.

In spite of the many hardships of life in Russia there are compensations. A peasant member of the Duma once told of the terrible condition of his own people, "their needs, their wants, their misery, their ignorance. All the same, we have great fun in our village; you ought to come and stay there. There is no such life in the world." Every village has its sunshine and laughter intermingled with its sorrows.

Recreational Life

Perhaps one reason for this is that the Russians have always been a singing people. They sing while they work and they sing while they play. The *balalaika,* a sort of triangular guitar, and the accordion are very popular. On Sundays and holidays the young men and girls go for festival walks to the accompaniment of this music. The main enjoyment seems to be playful conversation, music, and the out-of-doors. The Russian falls heir to a wealth of folk songs. There are historical epics, and lyrics of love, warfare, and death. There are nature songs welcoming back the sun after the winter, besides special ones for every festival.

On their gala days the Russians enjoy nothing better than singing and dancing. The girls often wear brilliantly colored costumes much adorned with embroidery and beading; these add to the picturesqueness of the dancing, which is both individual and social. The scene is one of rollicking fun and wholesome sociality. The Russian has a sense for dramatic art, and frequently the villagers will stage humorous dialogues. Festival days are so frequent and the Sabbath is so well observed that the peasants do have adequate recreation. Indeed, the Russian is probably far more socialized in this respect than the average American, whose amusements too often must center around the thrill of the unusual under circumstances which are not conducive to real re-creation.

Religion

The Greek Orthodox faith, the prevailing religion, by using elaborate ceremonial forms among an ignorant peasantry, has ministered to superstition, and helped to maintain the authority of the Tsar, who was the temporal head of the Church. Beautiful edifices have been built, with magnificent interiors, inspiring music, burning candles, and priests in golden robes, but almost nothing has been done in the way of social service. For the most part, the priests have not even dared to preach to the people, but have often served as secret agents for the Tsar. In the organization of reactionary parties, the church authorities have always played a part. It is natural that many Russians could not remain in this faith. Although theoretically there was religious freedom in Russia, practically there was not. Those who split from the Orthodox Church, whether Old Believers, Dukhobors, Molokans, Stundists or the followers of Sutaiev, were persecuted. Some of them were even driven from their villages and banished to Siberia. Tragic indeed are the stories of not a few of those who emigrated to America.

Education

In matters of education, the peasant has been worse off than in religion. In 1912, out of a population of one hundred and eighty millions, only seven were in school. Moreover, according to the report of the investigating committee of the third Duma, the educational influence which the schools exerted was insignificant. Many children, soon after leaving, were found to be practically illiterate—the terms were for only four or five months in the winter, anyway. It is no wonder that at least fifty per cent could not even sign their own names, and nearer seventy per cent could not read.

Even for the literate, only censored material was available. Not one word could be printed without being approved by the Tsar's appointee. Since the independent press followed the practice of leaving blank the parts deleted by the Government, often whole front page columns would be left with only here and there a sentence. This naturally made the thinking people deeply suspicious of the papers, the news, and the Government.

Relation to the Government

Nearly always where the peasant came in contact with the Government, the relationship was a harsh and disagreeable one. The *Ispravnik,* or police commissioner, had general supervision over each district. His will was law. He could fine or imprison any one he chose. Under him was the *Uriadnik,* or constable, who also had absolute power, subject to the disapproval of the *Ispravnik.* To make inspection he could enter any house at any time of day or night without a warrant. He could tear down an entire building if he claimed it did not meet the regulations. Besides these officials there was the *Zemsky Nachalnik*, who had administration over all the rural institutions and was higher than the *Uriadnik*. He could depose the elective officials of the peasant commune or *mir*, and order any peasant flogged. He belonged to the nobility and naturally would not betray their interests. There was only one way to placate an angry official in most of the villages and that was through bribery. Moreover, if an official wanted work done on his estate, the peasants would, of course, never dare to charge for it. They feared and hated the ordinary government official and tried to curry his favor on all occasions.

There was another way in which the peasant came into contact with the Government, and that was through the sale of *vodka*. The Government had a monopoly of its sale, and nearly one-third of the total state revenue was derived in this way. It was illegal to sell this liquor with an alcohol content of less than 40 per cent, and it might contain nearer 60 per cent. This did much to stultify any initiative which the peasant might have had, and to keep him in economic bondage.

Taxes were extremely heavy. In some cases they were more than the total income from the land. Yet since the village commune was responsible collectively for the payment of the tax, and the peasant could not by law leave his village without consent, he was hopelessly under bondage. Besides, there were officials who could flog and imprison the delinquent. Even after the redemption payments on land were canceled in 1905, the indirect taxes on tea, sugar, cotton, and other articles used by the peasants were increased until 60 per cent of the total national revenue was raised in this way.

Worst of all, the male peasant was compelled to serve five years in the army and, in case of hostilities, could be conscripted and plunged into the maelstrom of war over issues about which he knew little and cared less. It was thus, in the World War, that Russia mobilized sixteen million men. They were snatched from their homes, perhaps not to return even on furlough during three long years of war. They served at a wage of fifty *kopeks* (twenty-five cents) a month. They ate out of a common dish pan, seven soldiers dipping their wooden spoons into the same bowl for their noonday meal. There was little or no welfare work done for them—they died like flies. At home their wives struggled alone with the land, accepting without a murmur whatever came of sickness and death. Frequently for years they were entirely without word from their husbands, who might be alive or dead for all they knew. Yet in this war they were treated better than in any of the former wars by which Russia has been afflicted.

Summary of Environmental Conditions

We have examined briefly the European background of the Russian; let us sum up the main environmental conditions which might affect his conduct in America.

Centuries of agricultural labor had intensified his love for the land. In spite of hard and bitter conditions, he remained on the soil, but felt that he was being cheated out of the full product of his labor.

Conditions in industry were hard, but not as hurried and machine-like as in America. Often the worker became inoculated with socialistic and anarchistic ideas.

The communal land ownership, the close village life, and the continued restriction of individual initiative forced him more and more into coöperative effort.

The peasant lived in congested, unsanitary quarters, but these conditions were mitigated by his outdoor life.

He was used to a vegetarian diet of fresh farm products.

He had little experience with doctors and accepted those available without question.

The women worked equally hard with the men.

Recreation was wholesome and satisfied the impulse to sociality.

The church satisfied the mystical craving of the

masses, but was doing little social service work and was definitely linked up with the autocracy.

Schools were few and the masses were illiterate.

The government was such that the peasants lived in continual fear of the officials and, for the most part, suffered under and disliked the military service.

Such were the social conditions in the Tsar's régime which, during all his life, bound the mind of the Russian. He was the victim of religious intolerance, social inequality, economic discrimination, political despotism, and compulsory ignorance. While all these conditions made life uncomfortable, poverty was the most potent force in stimulating emigration.

Obstacles to Emigration

But America could claim only the more alert and forceful. For the masses, the difficulties that stood in the way were too great. For years the Government had feared greatly that Russians emigrating to foreign countries might get republican ideas. Emigration was a thing unknown to the Russian law and the adoption of foreign citizenship was illegal. The longest period for which a passport could be granted was five years, and this demanded special permission from the administrative department.

Later, however, in the reign of the last Tsar, the Government evidently decided that a sojourn in America would not necessarily result in republican ideas, for immigrants would see only the dark side.

In 1905 the chairman of the Council of the Tsar's Ministers, S. Witte, even said in a speech to the railroad workers, "Look on the republic of America, and you, gentlemen, will find that political liberty which prevails there always has served and will serve the interests of the rich, but not the proletariat."

Every emigrant, nevertheless, had to secure a special passport from the governor of the province. This meant filing an application which cost money. Furthermore, if the applicant was within three years of military age, it would be doubtful if his request would be granted. To leave the country illegally was possible, but this, again, meant the payment of a bribe to those who would make the arrangements. Even if able to leave, the trip to America cost nearly one hundred dollars, and this seemed an enormous sum to the poor peasant. Still, many did get away. The Jews came first, and their letters to friends about the wealth of America stimulated the peasants in the border states to try their fortune in this land of untold opportunity. There were three chief groups: the political refugees, or revolutionists, the unorthodox, who sought religious freedom, and the vast majority who came to make money and then return home, or at least to escape the poverty and injustice of Russia. There were still a few others who sought a new experience, exploration and adventure with new opportunities.

Characteristics of the Russian

Because of the conditions in his European background and because of certain racial traits, the Russian has come to America with other marked personal characteristics. Professor Etienne Antonelli, a political scientist of France, who has spent years in Russia, has summarized the thought of many Russian writers in the following:

1. The peasant has a predominance of feeling over will.
2. He does not perceive inconsistencies and is tolerant of ideas.
3. He has a horror of any kind of rule or any kind of compulsion.
4. He has little forethought and yields to the pleasure of the moment.
5. He feels that passion excuses everything.
6. He has no idea of parliamentary government and dislikes any kind of law.
7. He has intellectual curiosity.
8. He places the soul or personality above everything else, has a contempt for material things, and is incapable of strong hate.
9. He believes in humility. The individual should efface himself in all.

Some of these traits have been emphasized in Russian literature and unquestionably there is an element of truth in them, but their universal application is doubtful. For example, the peasant may hate laws and rules, but he certainly did not object very seriously to those imposed by the *mir*. Any list of characteristics must be incomplete and open to criticism, but the writer prefers to call attention to the following:

The Russian is very patient and stolid. He is willing to endure a good deal, even under bad conditions, and will work uncomplainingly for long hours at low wages. The peasant is thoroughly religious. In every home you see an ikon, or sacred picture. As to the church and the priest, he may or may not be skeptical, depending on his experience. His love of music and the theater is a well-known characteristic. He is very sympathetic, always willing to contribute to the need of those who are suffering. If a Russian is killed in a mine or factory, his neighbors will often care for the widow and children, though they themselves may barely be making a living. The peasant is naturally suspicious of strangers, the inevitable and bitter result of a long experience with those whom he regards as superiors. None the less, sociability is a marked trait. The Russian likes to talk by the hour to his friends and will share his last morsel of food, while he talks with a stranger. He is also quickly responsive to what strikes him as a higher good, and is willing to suffer for it. The long record of those who have died for their revolutionary ideals, and the larger number who have suffered for years in the Tsar's prisons is eloquent testimony to this trait.

Such, then, is the character of the Russian Slav

who comes to replenish the labor of our industrial army in factory, mine, and workshop. The impress of an autocratic Tsar's régime lies heavy upon these people. They come with a big handicap, but also with traits which are good. Many of them have the same longing for liberty that actuated our forefathers when they founded this republic. We should be ready to help them to understand and appreciate our democracy. Furthermore, America needs their labor, and if they can but be assimilated, they may well contribute to our welfare and happiness.

BIBLIOGRAPHY
ON
The Russians in America

I. Books, Public Documents and Pamphlets

Abbott, Grace, *The Immigrant and the Community*, New York. Century Co., 1917.

Antin, Mary, *The Promised Land*, Boston and New York: Houghton Mifflin Co., 1912.

Antin, Mary, *They Who Knock at Our Gates*, Boston and New York: Houghton Mifflin Co., 1914.

Balch, E. G., *Our Slavic Fellow Citizens*, New York: Charities Publication Committee, 1910.

Breckinridge, S. P., *New Homes for Old*, New York: Harper and Brothers Co., 1921.

Byington, M. F., *Homestead: The Households of a Mill Town*, New York: Charities Publication Committee, 1910.

California Commission of Immigration and Housing, *Report on an Experiment in Los Angeles in the summer of 1917 for Americanization of foreign-born women*, Sacramento: State Printing Office, 1917.

California Commission of Immigration and Housing, *Report of Fresno's Immigration Problem*, Sacramento: State Printing Office, 1917.

Commons, J. R., *Races and Immigrants in America*, New York: Macmillan Co., 1915.

Daniels, John, *America via the Neighborhood*, New York: Harper and Brothers Co., 1920.

Davis, M. M., Jr., *Immigrant Health and the Community*, New York: Harper and Brothers Co., 1921.

Dimock, L. A., *Comrades from Other Lands*, New York and Chicago: Fleming H. Revell Co., 1913.

Fitch, J. A., *The Steel Workers*, New York: Charities Publication Committee, 1910.

Grose, H. B., *Aliens or Americans?* New York: Missionary Education Movement, 1912.

Henry, J. R., *Some Immigrant Neighbors*, New York and Chicago: Fleming H. Revell Co., 1912.

Hodges, LeRoy, *Slavs on Southern Farms*, Washington: Government Printing Office, 1914. Senate Document, No. 595.

McClure, Archibald, *Leadership of the New America, Racial and Religious*, New York: George H. Doran Co., 1916.

Orth, S. P., *Our Foreigners; A Chronicle of Americans in the Making*, New Haven: Yale University Press, 1920.

Park, R. E., and Miller, H. A., *Old World Traits Transplanted,* New York: Harper and Brothers Co., 1920.

Prugavin, A S., *Religious Sects in New York,* Pamphlet in Russian.

Prugavin, A. S., *Die Inquisition der russisch orthodoxen Kirche,* Berlin: F. Gottheiner, 1905.

Ripley, W. Z., *The Races of Europe,* New York: D. Appleton and Co., 1899.

Roberts, Peter, *Immigrant Races in North America,* New York: Y. M. C. A. Press, 1910.

Roberts, Peter, *The New Immigration,* New York: Macmillan Co., 1912.

Ross, E. A., *The Old World in the New,* New York: Century Co., 1914.

Sheridan, F. J., *Italian, Slavic, and Hungarian Unskilled Immigrant Laborers in the United States,* Washington: Government Printing Office, 1907. Dept. of Labor Bulletin, vol. 15.

Slavic Alliance in Cleveland, Cleveland, 1904. Pamphlet in Russian.

Smith, R. K., *The People of the Eastern Orthodox Churches,* Springfield (Mass.), 1913.

Sokoloff, Alexis, *Mediaeval Russia,* New York: Survey Associates, 1914. Pittsburg Survey, vol. 6.

Sokaloff, Lillian, *Russians in Los Angeles,* University of Southern California, 1918. Publications in Sociology, no. 17.

Speek, P. A., *A Stake in the Land,* New York: Harper and Brothers Co., 1921.

Steiner, E. A., *The Broken Wall,* New York and Chicago: Fleming H. Revell Co., 1911.

Thompson, F. V., *Schooling of the Immigrant,* New York: Harper and Brothers Co., 1920.

Thompson, R. A., *The Russian Settlement in California Known as Fort Rosa,* Santa Rosa (Cal.): Sonoma Democrat Publishing Co., 1896. Pamphlet.

United States Bureau of the Census, *Thirteenth and Fourteenth Census,* Washington: Government Printing Office.

United States Bureau of Foreign and Domestic Commerce, *One Hundred Years of American Immigration,* Washington: Government Printing Office, 1919. Daily Consular and Trade Reports, No. 254.

United States Bureau of Foreign and Domestic Commerce, *Statistical Abstract of the United States, 1919,* Washington: Government Printing Office, 1920.

United States Bureau of Immigration, *Annual Reports of the Commissioner-General of Immigration to the Secretary of Labor,* 1910-20, Washington: Government Printing Office.

United States Immigration Commission, *Reports,* Washington: Government Printing Office, 1911. Vols. 1-42.

Van Kleeck, Mary, *Artificial Flower Makers,* New York: Survey Associates, 1913.

Warne, F. J., *The Immigrant Invasion,* New York: Dodd, Mead and Co., 1913.

Wright, C. D., *Influence of Trade Unions on Immigrants,* Washington: Government Printing Office, 1905. Department of Labor Bulletin, No. 56.

II. MAGAZINE ARTICLES

Ainsworth, F. H., "Are We Shouldering Europe's Burden?" *Charities, and the Commons,* vol. 12, pp. 134-5, February 6, 1904.

Balch, E. G., "Peasant Background of Our Slavic Fellow Citizens," *Survey,* vol. 24, pp. 666-77, August 6, 1910.

Boas, Franz, "Race Problems in America," *Science,* vol. 29, pp. 839-49, May 28, 1909.

Boeckh, Richard, "The Determination of Racial Stock Among American Immigrants," *Quarterly Publications of the American Statistical Association,* vol. 10, pp. 199-221, December, 1906.

Bolonski, J. R., "Poolrooms or Schoolrooms for Russians in America," *Survey,* vol. 44, pp. 519-20, July 17, 1920.

Cance, Alexander, "Slav Farmers on the 'Abandoned Farm' Area of Connecticut," *Survey,* vol. 27, pp. 951-6, October 7, 1911.

Cance, Alexander, "Immigrant Rural Communities," *Annals of the American Academy of Political and Social Science,* vol. 40, pp. 69-80, March, 1912.

Claghorn, K. H., "Immigration in Its Relation to Pauperism," *Annals of the American Academy of Political and Social Science,* vol. 24, pp. 187-205, July, 1904.

Claghorn, K. H., "Our Immigrants and Ourselves," *Atlantic Monthly,* vol. 86, pp. 535-48, October, 1900.

Commons, J. R., "Race Composition of the American People," *Chautauquan,* vol. 38, pp. 33-42, 118-25, 223-34, 333-40, 433-43, 533-43; vol. 39, pp. 13-22, 115-24, 217-25, September, 1903-May, 1904.

Commons, J. R., "Slavs in the Bituminous Mines of Illinois," *Charities and the Commons,* vol. 13, pp. 227-9, December 3, 1904.

Commons, J. R., "Wage Earners of Pittsburg," *Charities and the Commons,* vol. 21, pp. 1051-64, March 6, 1909.

Durand, E. D., "Our Immigrants and the Future," *World's Work,* vol. 23, pp. 431-43, February, 1912.

Elkinton, Joseph, "The Dukhobors," *Charities and the Commons,* vol. 13, pp. 252-6, December 3, 1904.

Fetler, William, "Russians in the United States," *Missionary Review of the World,* vol. 38, pp. 923-8, December, 1915.

Fleming, W. L., "Immigration to the Southern States," *Political Science Quarterly*, vol. 20, pp. 276-97, June, 1905.

Foster, Maximilian, "The Citizen," *Everybody's*, vol. 19, pp. 628-40, November, 1908.

Gruszczynski, Maxim, "Russian Immigrant on American Continent," *Pan-American Magazine*, vol. 26, pp. 29-34, November, 1917.

Henry, J. R., "Do Russians Make Good American Citizens?" *World Outlook*, vol. 6, pp. 14-15, May, 1920.

Hine, L. W., "Immigrant Types in the Steel Districts," *Charities and the Commons*, vol. 21, pp. 581-8, January 2, 1909.

Hrdlicka, Ales, "The Slavs," *Czecho-Slovak Review*, vol. 2, pp. 180-187, November, 1918.

Hughes, Elizabeth, "Chicago Housing Conditions," *American Journal of Sociology*, vol. 20, pp. 289-312, November, 1914.

Kellogg, P. U., "The McKee's Rocks Strike," *Survey*, vol. 22, pp. 656-65, August 7, 1909.

Kellor, F. A., "Protection of Immigrant Women," *Atlantic Monthly*, vol. 101, pp. 246-55, February, 1908.

Koukol, A. B., "The Slav's a Man for a' That," *Charities and the Commons*, vol. 21, pp. 589-98, January 2, 1909.

Lauck, W. J., "The Bituminous Coal Miner and Coke Worker of Western Pennsylvania," *Survey*, vol. 26, pp. 34-51, April 1, 1911.

Lee, Joseph, "Assimilation and Nationality," *Charities and the Commons*, vol. 19, pp. 1453-55, January 25, 1908.

Literary Digest, "Russians in America," vol. 63, p. 41, November 29, 1919.

Lloyd, J. A. T., "Teuton versus Slav," *Fortnightly Review*, vol. 105, pp. 883-93, May, 1916.

Lovejoy, O. R., "The Slav Child: A National Asset or a Liability," *Charities and the Commons*, vol. 14, pp. 882-4, July 1, 1905.

McLaughlin, Allan, "The Slavic Immigrant," *Popular Science Monthly*, vol. 63, pp. 25-32, May, 1903.

Mayo-Smith, Richmond, "Theories of Mixtures of Races and Nationalities," *Yale Review*, vol. 3, pp. 166-186, August, 1894.

Miller, H. A., "The Lost Division," *Survey*, vol. 40, pp. 307-9, June 15, 1918.

Moravsky, M., "Greenhorn in America," *Atlantic Monthly*, vol. 122, pp. 663-9, November, 1918.

Norton, E. S., "The Need of a General Plan for Settling Immigrants Outside the Great Cities," *Charities and the Commons*, vol. 12, pp. 152-4, February 6, 1904.

Outlook, "Russian Immigrant and His Savings," vol. 114, p. 13, September 6, 1916.

Parker, E. H., "Russians in Business," *Chamber's Journal*, pp. 103-6, February, 1915.

Ripley, W. Z., "Race Factors in Labor Unions," *Atlantic Monthly*, vol. 93, pp. 299-308, March, 1904.

Ripley, W. Z., "The European Population of the United States," *Journal of the Royal Anthropological Institute of Great Britain and Ireland,* vol. 28, pp. 221-40, 1908.

Roberts, Peter, "The New Pittsburgers: Slavs and Kindred Immigrants in Pittsburg," *Charities and the Commons,* vol. 21, pp. 533-52, January 2, 1909.

Ross, E. A., "Slavs in America," *Century Magazine,* vol. 88, pp. 590-8, August, 1914.

Sayles, M. B., "Housing and Social Conditions in a Slavic Neighborhood," *Charities and the Commons,* vol. 13, pp. 257-61, December 3, 1904.

Smith, R. D., "Some Phases of the McKee's Rocks Strike," *Survey,* vol. 23, pp. 38-45, October 2, 1909.

Sokoloff, Alexis, "Old Believers," *Survey,* vol. 33, pp. 145-51, November 7, 1914.

Steiner, E. A., "From the Lovezin to Guinea Hill," *Outlook,* vol. 89, pp. 247-52, May 30, 1908.

Steiner, E. A., "The Foreign Born Population of the United States," *Scientific Monthly,* vol. 8, pp. 380-3, April, 1919.

Survey, "Russians in American Schools," vol. 44, p. 590, August 2, 1920.

Survey, "United for Freedom at Home," vol. 40, p. 292, June 8, 1918.

Townley-Fullam, C., "Pan-Slavism in America," *Forum,* vol. 52, pp. 177-85, August, 1914.

Tridon, A., "Russian Baiting in Our Ports," *Public,* vol. 21, pp. 698-700, June 1, 1918.

Wilson, H. L., and Smith, E. W., "Chicago Housing Conditions Among Slovaks," *American Journal of Sociology,* vol. 20, pp. 145-169, September, 1914.

Wing, M. T. C., "The Flag at McKee's Rocks," *Survey,* vol. 23, pp. 45-6, October 2, 1909.

Woolston, Florence, "Slavs in the United States," *Technical World,* pp. 135-44, October, 1911.